Sammy and Sunny

Sammy and Sunny

The Story of Hedvig Samuelson, Murdered by Winnie Ruth Judd

and

The Story of Sunny Worel's Search for Sammy

by

Sunny Lynn Worel

and

Janet V. Worel

Dedicated to the memory of:

Hedvig (Sammy) Samuelson (1903-1931)

and

Sunny Lynn Worel (1968-2014)

Two adventurous women who died too young

TABLE OF CONTENTS

Foreword

A Memory of Sunny

by Charles Kelly

Sunny Worel transcended time. Trained as a medical librarian, she used her training and skills to return to a world that had existed many years before she lived: the world of her great-aunt, Hedvig "Sammy" Samuelson. Sunny was on a mission to rescue the admirable life led by her great-aunt, a much-beloved schoolteacher and adventurer, from the way that life ended on Oct. 16, 1931, as part of a tabloid murder case.

In that, Sunny succeeded, as you will see in this book created by her mother, Janet Worel, much of it consisting of Sunny's accounts of her own travels.

Sunny had a unique set of skills. She was a detective of history, able to tease out the most obscure details from an old photograph, a brief diary entry, a tossed-off line in a letter written long ago. She was also an artist. She could use a small camera to compose a striking photo from the angles of a discarded metal chair, the turn of a snowdrift, the sweep of a bird in flight. She knew the names of things: bunchberry, lupine, ptarmigan, forget-me-not.

She loved to track down and watch movies from the 1930s—*Just Imagine, Peach O'Reno, Half Shot at Sunrise.* The old-time comic team of Wheeler and Woolsey was one of her favorites. She was intrigued by old novels that Sammy had read, such as *Ex-Wife* by Ursula Parrott and *The Yellow Mistletoe.* She knew the fashions and machinery of a forgotten age: the cloche hat, the beaded chiffon dress, the Jackson Bell radio.

My first contact with Sunny occurred in 2000, when I was working as a reporter for *The Arizona Republic.* At the time, I was assigned to a section of the paper called Arizona Diary. Sunny called from her home in Minneapolis, wanting to place an article in the section about her research into the life of Sammy, who had been one of two victims of the 1931 Winnie Ruth Judd Trunk Murder Case in Phoenix. That effort did not work out, but Sunny would get back in touch with me from time to time in the ensuing years as she continued her investigations in Phoenix. We became friends and often talked on the phone. I sometimes helped her with her work. She was as fine a researcher as I have ever known.

Sunny was never happier than when analyzing and re-analyzing a neglected clue or a puzzling sequence of events in Sammy's life, of trying to see a pattern others had glossed over. In doing that, she was incredibly thorough and insightful. In this quest, she found meaning, and in finding meaning, she found happiness.

She was a beautiful woman and a clever one. She did what she set out to do.

PREFACE

By Sunny Lynn Worel and Janet V. Worel

I stand in a dark corridor.

Ahead, I see a vague figure moving quickly through a passage. The only faint light in the corridor comes from the body of a woman. I pursue her slowly at first, then faster. She remains ahead of me, just out of reach. Laughter fills the corridor.

She pauses and I approach her. I see her in more detail now. Suddenly she begins to glow more intensely. I shout, "Sammy!" She looks at me for a brief moment as if surprised and smiles. She flares into blinding light. I scream. She vanishes. Everything goes black.

I stand in a dark corridor.

October 16 - I wake with a start. The room is black since it is still dawn. I examine the shadows on the wall and ceiling with suspicion. The familiar chocolate lab lies stretched out across the end of the bed, unbothered.

I rise and look around. I snap on the light only to find nothing. The Labrador rolls over onto her back, opening her right eye to peek at me.

I wander around the apartment aimlessly looking for something. There is nothing unusual. I consider the dream. I confirm that the door is locked and head back to bed.

I see the book on the floor with a trunk on the cover. A limp, hand dangling from its slightly opened lid adorns the dust jacket. Bloody, pink pajamas hang from the opening. I turn off the light tentatively and climb under the warm comforter. Mahogany creeps up the side of the bed and inserts her head onto my shoulder. I automatically stroke her back. "Good girl," I say unconsciously, "Good dog."

I lie in bed until the sun rises. I study the brilliant red maple through the slats in the blinds. I could not believe that 70 years had passed.

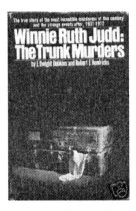

I was 5 years old when the first Winnie Ruth Judd book was published by Dobkins and Hendricks in 1973. The book tells one version of the crime in which Winnie Ruth Judd shot her two friends, packed their bodies into trunks and shipped them off to Los Angeles on a train. It was one of the most publicized murder cases in Arizona history. The black dust jacket portrayed a gruesome picture of a steamer trunk with a pair of pink pajamas draped over the edge of the slightly opened lid. A limp, lifeless hand dangles out of the opening. The picture on the book made quite an impression on my young mind. Hedvig (Sammy) Samuelson, my great aunt, was one of the women in the trunks. This is the only way I ever thought of her as a child. She was the body in the trunk. Since the family had always been remarkably silent about Sammy, my mother

4

and her sisters bought copies of this first Winnie Ruth Judd book. They were understandably curious. One of my aunts wrote to Sammy's brother Arnold, asking about the crime. He replied by sending back an audio tape criticizing her for her "blood thirsty interest" in the Winnie Ruth Judd murder case. Arnold explained that the case flared up in the papers and stayed there. It disrupted the family. Every time he picked up the newspaper or turned on the radio, he had to read or hear an account of the murder of his favorite sister. If this were not bad enough, friends would approach and ask him questions about the crime. Arnold complained that the treatment of the press towards his sister was always that of the victim, the butchered corpse. He claimed the press had no sensitivity for the personality involved. For these reasons, the family took "the stiff arm" and never spoke much of Sammy. The only thing the family could do was "to survive and get their minds on to other things". Sammy's character got lost somewhere between the headlines. Few had ever written about her as she really was.

I realized that there was much more to know about Sammy Samuelson after visiting her first cousin Inga Betten in Palatine, Illinois in early 1998. The 94 year-old woman gave me several photographs of Sammy. One was a postcard of Sammy standing in an Alaskan field adorned in a coat made of animal skins. The card said, "Christmas Greetings from Hedvig Samuelson" in a very fancy script. She appeared so happy and vibrant. She took me in. I wanted to know more about her, not about the crime, but about her.

Very few things remained seventy years after Sammy's death. Back home in Minnesota, the family had dozens of photographs of her.

Many of these pictures were from the homestead near White Earth, North Dakota where she spent her childhood. There were several compelling pictures of her in Juneau, Alaska where she taught school in the late twenties. There was a picture of her dressed in a Japanese kimono, playing the role of Yum-Yum in Gilbert and Sullivan's, *The Mikado*. A scrapbook was filled with newspaper clippings about the crime. I noticed a newspaper article with entries lifted from Sammy's personal diary.

I started to inquire about this diary. Obtaining the diary seemed to be the perfect way to resurrect the personality of Sammy Samuelson. Newspapers related that the prosecuting attorney, Lloyd Andrews, took this diary with him to Los Angeles during the initial investigation.[1] Another source stated that the well-known photographer E.D. Newcomer stole this diary from the girls' home. According to the story, Newcomer entered the duplex where the girls were murdered, took the diary and as many photos as he could find, and waited for the police to arrive.[2] Jana Bommersbach in her book, The Trunk Murderess, stated that one of the lawyers concealed the diary. It contained incriminating evidence against several men in the Phoenix area.[3] From several newspaper articles, I pieced together some of the diary entries. The diary has not been recovered.

---

[1] *Slayer Still Free Despite Wide Dragnet*, in *Grand Forks Herald*, October 22, 1931: Grand Forks, ND, p. 1.

[2] Johnson, Burke, *He was There: Arizona Republic Presents and Exhibit of Photographs 1928-1968* by *E. D. Newcomer*, in *Arizona Historical Foundation*, 1971:Phoenix, p. 5.

[3] Bommersbach, Jana, *The Trunk Murderess: Winnie Ruth Judd*, Simon & Schuster: 1992.

I retraced the many miles Sammy covered in her life. As a single woman in the Twenties, she traveled about the country independently by train and boat. She taught school in North Dakota, Montana, and Alaska. She worked two summers for the park service at Yellowstone National Park and at Mount McKinley Park in the interior of Alaska. She visited remote islands in British Columbia. For health reasons, she moved to Phoenix, Arizona after she contracted a severe case of tuberculosis. Over the years, all of these places were my destinations. Sammy had left small personal things behind for me to discover, things from which I could tell her story in a book. (Sunny Worel, great niece of Sammy Samuelson and daughter of Janet and Jack Worel)

Out of these discoveries, Sunny had hopes of writing a book that portrayed an accurate narrative of Sammy's life. She considered her research on Sammy her most important life work. She became enthralled with the 20's and 30's, loved art deco and often dressed and furnished her house to fit that era. About the time that she felt her research was complete and the book could be written, Sunny was diagnosed with Stage 4 colon cancer in February of 2012. This resulted in a tough battle which took much of her energy and the writing project took a back seat. She spent much of the rest of her life seeking treatment options through many clinical trials after her other treatment possibilities ran out. Although the book was written in her head, she neither found the time nor energy to put it on paper.

Sunny died on July 1, 2014. Her parents were left to sort through the remnants of her life. Among these were travel diaries, notes, clippings and pictures related to her research on Sammy. I, her mother and the niece of Sammy Samuelson, who had peripherally followed her journey, grieved for the loss of my wonderful daughter, and also despaired that her life work had not been completed. After making decisions about such things as her house, clothes and other of life's accumulated possessions, I was left with the Sammy research. Much of it was related to Winnie Ruth Judd and the crime itself. I decided to seek the help of others to place this part in archives. Then I was left with the information about Sammy herself, not as the crime victim, but Sammy as a personality. I at first thought the task of writing a book about her was daunting. I am not a writer and have never aspired to be such. After a time of sifting through Sunny's travel diaries, her time line of Sammy's life, files in her computer, notes in tablets made to herself, etc., I found that she had basically written the book herself. My job became easier; that of a compiler; an organizer. This book that resulted is primarily from Sunny's own words that I have arranged in a manner that made sense to me. I have added information about the Samuelson family of which I have knowledge, have paraphrased some of Sunny's notes and added filler material, but this is Sunny's book and she is the primary author. I soon found that the book I compiled was not only about Sammy, but equally important was the portrayal of Sunny and her diligent pursuit of the Sammy story. The personalities of both women become revealed. I am not sure what Sunny's book would have included, but I hope that this would meet with her approval and cause her to smile. Hopefully, Sammy would smile as well! Writing this has put purpose into my grieving over Sunny. Through this I have become even more aware of how remarkable, clever, smart and adventurous both Sammy and Sunny were. I celebrate both of their short lived lives.

(Janet V. Worel, Sunny's mother and Sammy's niece)

CHAPTER One: White Earth, N.D.

BIRDS-EYE VIEW, WHITE EARTH, N.D. NO. 1.

WHITE EARTH IS A city in Mountrail County, North Dakota, in the far northwest part of the state. It was founded in 1888. The town's population was about 250 in the 1920s when Sammy lived there, had shrunk to about 63 when Sunny visited in 2000, but now has increased to over 500 in 2015 due to the oil boom.

Sammy lived in White Earth

Sarah Hedvig (Sammy) Samuelson was born on Nov. 17, 1903, in Milwaukee, Wisconsin, at her parent's rental house at 645 Washington Street. Carrie Gabrielson served as attendant or midwife. Sammy, as she will be referred to throughout this book, was the third of the four Samuelson children, preceded by Anna, born in 1898, and by Samuel, born in 1900. The picture of the house shows Samuel revisiting the house as a grown man.

Sammy was born to Anders and Marie Samuelson, both rather recent Norwegian immigrants who met in Milwaukee and married in 1897. Anders worked for his brother Andreas in the sailing business on the Great Lakes, sailing on the boat the *Stafford* and supplemented his income by working as a night watchman in the winter. Still, income

was unsteady and life was economically difficult. With the arrival of the new baby, Sammy, Anders made the decision to try farming instead. He had heard of free land farther west if one used the Homestead Act.

Anders worked hard to save money during the sailing season of 1904. Early in September of that year, he took the Great Northern train alone from Milwaukee to Minneapolis and then on to Minot, North Dakota. From there, with advice from the land office, he took the train farther west to White Earth, the only place where the locomotive could stop for water between Minot and Williston. He explored the area, and found an available area six miles south of the town that he thought would be ideal. After finding a man to survey it, he secured the legal description of the land and applied to claim it in Minot on his journey by train back to Milwaukee.

By April, 1905, Anders retraced his trip to White Earth and built a sod house with a couple of rooms against a hill. By late May, Marie arrived with the three children and a load of furniture aboard the train. Sammy was then about 1 ½ years old. It must have been a long tedious ride for them all. Shortly after the family had settled in, rain seeped into the crude house and soaked the furniture. Tar paper was placed over the

beds and more sod used to reinforce the roof and the walls. Soon after, Anders discovered that his land description was incorrect and that he had filed for worthless land instead of the prime section on which he had

SCENE ON FARM OF A. S. SAMUELSON, WHITE EARTH, N. D.

built. Luckily, no one else had claimed the land he wanted, and he was able to correct the mistake. That summer Anders bought a pair of oxen and began breaking the land. He called his farm Håland after his family farm in Norway. Marie and the children met the few neighbors and tried to store up enough food to survive the winter. Anders also needed to build a small barn to shelter the oxen. There were only two rooms in the sod house: a main room and a sleeping room shared by all members of the family. For warmth, they acquired a stove and burned buckets of dried cow dung donated by neighbors.

Somehow that first winter passed and Anders planted flax and later wheat. During the next five years, he was able to fulfill the requirements needed to finally own the land and paid off the

homestead fees in full. He built a house with plastered walls and a sturdy roof and later made additions to the dwelling. The family had 40 fenced-in acres and three wells.

Through the early years they enjoyed ideal wheat farming weather, including regular rains.

Sammy, Anna and Sam were growing and thriving on the prairie. They first attended school in various homes, where parents tried to teach them what they knew. Then the community hired a school teacher who came to the homes until a school house

was built. Later the Samuelson children attended the nearby Hanson

School, where 10 children were taught by a teacher responsible for all the grades. Sam is on the far right in this picture, Anna is third from the right standing, and Sammy is sitting second to the right in the first row.

Church was similar to the school in the beginning. Families would meet in different homes where children had a chance to see each other as well as to take part in some sort of Sunday school. A parent often had to take the place of the minister by reading from the Bible. Actual ministers would come when they could – sometimes on skis in the winter. The Samuelsons' favorite was Rev. Aune. Church became an all-day social affair. Everyone contributed food for a meal and it was great fun for all. The Presbyterian Church was later used by community residents for their Norwegian Lutheran services and also as a school house. Revival meetings were sometimes held, occasionally in the coulee near the Samuelsons' house in the summer.

Although life was good, Marie at times felt isolated on the prairie. She sorely missed her family and a more established church. In the winter of 1911, Marie packed up the three children and took the train to Milwaukee for a visit. She had a sister, Thrine Nelson, there and the

children could meet their cousins: Alice, Ida and Thelma. This must have been an exciting time for seven-year- old Sammy. Fifty-two year old Anders remained alone on the

prairie. He suffered from varicose veins, arthritis and rheumatism, and was fatigued from the heavy farm labor, so perhaps he welcomed the time alone to rest. He was proficient at baking bread and was self-sufficient. To occupy his time, he enjoyed making rag rugs from old clothing scraps.

Forty-year-old Marie was pregnant at the time of the trip to Milwaukee. After her return, on the very cold night of Feb. 6, 1912, Arnold Morris came into the world in their house on the prairie. Anders took his horse and buggy and fetched Cecilia Olson, a neighbor a few miles away, to serve as midwife. Recovery was slow for Marie, and Arnold was colicky. Neither was doing well so arrangements were made with a family in White Earth to take Marie and Arnold in for about a month until the weather improved. Anders cared for the other children at home.

The summer of 1912 was favorable for the Samuelsons and they were able to expand their holdings. Anders' sister Sarah Tobine, who had

attempted to homestead on a nearby plot, was unable to tolerate prairie life and had been unable to find a husband, so she sold her land to Anders and left. A small hut on her former property was hauled a half-mile to their house and attached to it. Anna and Sammy now had an area for their own bedroom. The weather had been excellent for wheat farming that summer and the harvest was profitable. Marie began to think about the upcoming winter with the new baby. She worried that the schools were inadequate for the children. Usually the school teacher, who taught eight grades, had only an eighth-grade education herself. Marie wanted better schooling for her children. She and Anna rode into Williston and located a house that they could rent. Anders agreed to the plan but told her he would only be able to visit them since he had to stay on their place and look after the animals.

They needed to find some used furniture for the rented house in Williston. They didn't need much, because the house was more like a shed, with only one bedroom for the five of them. Marie was able to wash clothes in the kitchen sink and hang them in an unfinished attic upstairs. There was an outhouse behind the house, which was at 611 Seventh Ave. W., a block from West Lawn School.

A Lutheran church was also nearby. Sammy and Sam were enrolled in the elementary school, which Anna also attended until the high school term started in January. At the high school, Anna was able to take extremely difficult subjects, such as trigonometry. This proved hard for Anna, but Marie was very proud of her accomplishments and that she was planning to become a teacher. Sam did well, too, but had to miss school often since Anders needed him to help on the farm. Sam fell behind and was sixteen before he finished the eighth grade. Sammy was a good student and also thought she might like teaching, or perhaps nursing. While the children were in school, Marie was home with Arnold, and found time to take him with her frequently to church gatherings. This arrangement worked well and, most years, they continued to rent the house during the school year through 1919. The children were being properly educated and Marie liked it in town, but the arrangement did drain the profits from the farm.

Sammy was mentioned in the Williston School paper for being proficient in handwriting. More frequently, she attended the schools in White Earth. The paper in White Earth ran school news and Sammy's name often appeared for good attendance and good grades. She was recognized for her singing and frequently was the soloist at special events. She won a testament at a church contest where she sang a chorus from memory after the pastor had sung a verse of it on the previous evening. As a ninth grader, she was regularly attending the White Earth School, where she was listed as the treasurer of the Excelsior Literary Society. As part of the literary club, she participated in a Thanksgiving program and in a George Washington pageant the following February. In 1918, Sammy joined the Red Cross to help support the servicemen from that area who were fighting in World War 1.

At some point in her sophomore year in high school, Sammy attended South Division High School in Milwaukee. She lived with Thrine Nelson at 655 Twenty-Seventh Ave. and enjoyed spending time with her cousins Alice, Ida and Thelma. Marie had taken Sammy along with her for a prolonged visit with her relatives. Whenever Marie visited either Milwaukee or Chicago, Sammy went with her and attended school wherever she was.

In the first picture, Sammy is visiting her aunt Bertina in Chicago. Bertina is on the far right, Sammy is next to her and the others are her cousins. Another Chicago visit shows Sammy with Marie visiting her sister Anna. Anna's children are Betty, sitting in the center, Ruth, seated to the right, and Anna Mae, who is being held by Marie.

By 1919, the family no longer rented the house in Williston. Marie was satisfied that there were other options for the children's education. Anna had already graduated from Williston High School, and Sam was attending the Agricultural School in Grand Forks to catch up with his studies. He was graduated from there in 1921. Sammy was the only one who graduated from the White Earth High School. Arnold struggled behaviorally at the White Earth School, but managed to graduate in good standing from the nearby Tioga High School. In June of 1919, Sammy performed a vocal solo for the graduation exercises at White Earth although she was not graduating that year. She may have boarded some of this time with people in White Earth since it was noted in the local paper that on Feb. 15, 1919, she had spent Saturday at the home of her parents. This would not have been newsworthy if she was living there all the time.

Sammy graduated from the White Earth High School on June 1, 1922, in a class of five. She gave the class Salutatory. The Class Motto was "Finished, yet Beginning," the Class Colors were Red and White, and the Class Flower was a red rose.

Pictures reveal some of Sammy's life at home, where her family adored her. After the Samuelsons' acquired a car it was sometimes used as an extra room to entertain friends. The following are pictures of the Samuelson family on the farm.

Marie was proud that the children were educated, thriving and now becoming independent. However, life was getting difficult on the farm for her and Anders. They had saved no money during the earlier years. Besides the expense of the extra rental home, the family spent more money when Marie traveled with Sammy to Chicago or Milwaukee. Marie was less able to do this in the 1920s. Up to that

point, rains had been plentiful and farming, though difficult, had brought in money. As the Twenties progressed, less and less rain fell, and drought conditions were the norm. Anders began to borrow money and put mortgages on the farm and on the land received from Sarah Tobine. A couple of good farming years would repay the debts, he reasoned. However, things didn't work out. With little money, Marie worried along with Anders about what would happen to them. Anders was suddenly an old man, unable to cope well with farming. He had developed rheumatism and was having trouble walking. Also, his eyesight was failing: he had cataracts in both eyes. As the 1920s advanced, the general economy began to fail, and it dragged the aging Samuelsons down with it. In 1928 the bank began to foreclose on part of their property. In 1931, the bank took the rest of their property in foreclosure. Marie and Anders didn't know where to turn. They simply remained on the farm since no one else had money to buy it.

Worse was to come. A minister accompanied by several people from White Earth came to the house late in October of 1931 and told Marie and Anders that their precious daughter Hedvig (Sammy) had been murdered. This was the devastating final blow that forced them off the land. Sam and his wife Hilda, along with Arnold, drove out and took them to Minneapolis. They had to leave most of their possessions behind. They could only take what they could fit in the small car occupied by five people. The neighbors took in the animals. But this is getting ahead of our story about Sammy.

Arnold visits White Earth

Sammy's brother Arnold returned to White Earth in the summer of 1932 after his parents had left. He was a recent graduate of the University of Minnesota in journalism and was still reeling from the blow he also experienced in losing Sammy. He was restless and decided to hitchhike about that summer. Arnold kept a diary of his travels he called *Post Graduate Vagabonding*. Excerpts from this diary reveal this visit:

"The old place was deserted. Rather dreary and forsaken looking, quiet as a tomb. The grass was grown tall in the yard. Weeds were knee high. Just the same, the old home has a fascination for me. I walked through the empty, dust ridden rooms and began sweeping. I would resume sleeping in my bedroom. The kerosene stove, cooking utensils, the beds, bureau, the table and book case were left. It would suffice for batching. The house stimulates memories of olden days. I can picture all of the folks doing various things about the place. It is hard to realize Dad isn't here. With borrowed bedclothes and chair, I moved over the second night. It was lonely, and I craved Pup's company. Before retiring, I visited Alf and his mother. Returning home I missed the light in the window that used to await me no matter what hour I came. It was dark, so that light should be there, I thought. When I dismounted, I half-way expected Dad to come out and greet me from the doorway. But he didn't come. The picture I form of Dad here bears little resemblance with that of him in Minneapolis. Here he is the master of a household, bewildered, old, but spry and determined. He has not yet given up the ghost. The creaking of the shanty door had a familiar sound as I entered. The touch of the doorknob was as distinctive as ever. Even the slam of the door touches off many memories. The house is a vault of memories, and it is thereby rendered sacred to me, although under scrutiny of a casual observer it may be classified as a weather beaten shack that should be torn down."

"Every time I look out a window, I see one of the 8 or 9 farmhouses in view. They remind me of people. Traffic on the highways and farmers in the fields all tend to denote one's situation to the neighborhood. The old place fails to give the seclusion I crave. Only at night do I feel perfectly at ease. I'd rather have a hut down in the coulees where humanity is not in evidence, where the callers would be infrequent and welcome. Their trouble to drive this far out of the way would prove they really want to see me.

Mrs. Schmidt said I could use the tent. I, with Alf's team and wagon, moved the tent and all my belongings, including the furniture, down into the coulee. Moving was somewhat more adventurous than I'd anticipated. Half way down the steep hill, one of the neck yoke clasps came off and the wheels shoved against the rump of the old white mare. With a horse of any spirit, such an accident would have caused a runaway. But she fought the wagon back till the load was again on the level. In order to get down here, it was necessary to go over a lot of rough and stony country. In several places the road was dangerously on a slant. Ideal for a tip over. In the coulee I was forced to drive over a long stretch of big rocks. On this adventure I experienced some of the thrill of pioneer voyages, and I regretted that pioneering days are gone. The location for the tent is ideal. It stands on the bottom of a steep hill from which a cascading spring flows. The tent is shaded by large trees and cannot be seen from any direction until one is almost upon it. Still, it is only a dozen feet from the spring. On the other side is the open vale, which affords grass in abundance for Dude. The valley forms a natural corral, with ample grazing space. On one side is a high hill with a fence along it. On the other the brush is so thick

except for a few openings, and the bank so steep, a horse would not attempt to climb out. Below the tent, the side is well fenced by the branch dams which have mired the water. I keep the milk ice cold in the spring and wash my dishes there. In the morning, a nice cold bath. The isolation here is as complete as one may have in this country. I've never really lived before. All these 20 years I've been dead. This has been the most perfect day of my life!

How sweet this solitude beside a beautiful spring is! I awoke at 8 when the sun blazed in at me through the window, prepared a breakfast of eggs, potatoes, bread and milk, and set the dishes in the spring, where the running water washed them. I read poetry this morning and in the afternoon began an uninterrupted reading of <u>Le Miserable</u>, by Victor Hugo, which I think is excellent. I took an hour's nap at 3 and continued reading in the shade outside after awakening. When returned with the milk, I made a fire in the moonlight and ate another supper of baked potatoes, eggs, and bread. I got a big thrill out of the meal and watched the fire until 12 o'clock. Any shack I build will certainly have a fireplace. Everything is so perfect here, it seems unnatural. If this is life, then life can certainly be made enjoyable. Heaven is not preferred by this boy."

Sunny visits White Earth

Sunny visited White Earth as well on 9/11/2000, searching for traces of Sammy and recounted this in her travel diary:

The town of White Earth

"Despairingly quiet. The wind is raucous and the loudest thing here. I met two huskies and three horses – all friendly. No people. Two trains went by. I am sitting in the tall grass by the school. I wish that I wasn't so drowsy. I think I would like to sleep in the coulee if I could find the correct place. The school building is more of a dump now with deserted cars all around. I knew that I was trespassing, but I hope nobody cares. This is not the original school. I bet I could find out, but not now. I bought some XTC (energy drink) in Tioga. It seemed an unlikely place to buy such an item, but perhaps it will wake me up. I wonder if this barn like building next to the school is the gym. I bet so.

I was sitting down in the Centennial Park when the train came through. It couldn't be seen, but I imagined that this has been a common experience during the last 100 years.

Anders moved the family out here 95 years ago. It seems like a long time ago.

The horses behind the city hall are staring at me as if they have never seen people before.

I hear nothing but the wind. I can't even imagine that this ever was a bustling community, but I guess it was at some point.

The horse seems to want to jump the fence to approach me. Perhaps he has had too many rats (I mean oats) today. I would still like to nap here. I wonder if anyone would notice. It's pretty unusual to think about how tired and how much back pain I have had in the last few days. I am sick of driving! I hope nobody cares if I lay here a spell.

The ground is uneven here. The leaves are turning a bit in the valley. It's pretty "bumpy" landscape after coming down off the hill. It is unbelievably windy!"

The Homestead

"I walked from the road where the Fells now live. I walked until the land sloped down severely at a ditch. There seems to be an artificial bump by the ditch. If the property would be that tiny it would be the SE corner of the middle of the east end. Dad said it sloped down at the edge. I don't know but that artificial bump looks suspicious to me. Perhaps the sod house was there and the first house on top of the hill. Arnold said they moved the house after the barn blew down. Then I would suspect they moved it down by the road. I got another a good feeling down by a mound of rocks on the SW corner of the property. I

wonder if this is where Sammy reared her horse on the rocks. She is older in that picture. I can see the tree she was hugging on to while she is wearing that white dress being down here. I think that I would like to try camping again tonight. Maybe I will try the State Park. I am too chicken to trespass and sleep on the homestead property. There are sticky bushes with green and purple berries near the rock where I am perched. I am in-between the artificial looking hill and downhill from a natural looking hill. I wonder if I am even close. My legs are severely scratched from the crop remains and these woody berry bushes. I will be feeling the sting of that for a while.

Still no presence. I guess I was suspecting something.

Arnold said the first house was where the pasture was later. I think that would put it close to where I am, being the property was this long.

Crickets are loud back here. Especially in the ditch. There is a purple vetch growing. Small cottonwoods are in the ditch. There is a circular ditch, like a small lake to my SE. There is no water in there now.

There are many rocks. Apparently the bigger ones were moved into piles; although there are smaller white rocks scattered about. I can see #2 Highway from here. Although that road was rerouted, I feel a bit too close to it. It is cold now that the sun went behind a cloud. It is still windy. It is dry however and I doubt if it will rain. I am in a cow pasture with a bunch of black cows. Three stared at me intently. Ah, the sun. Still wishing for confirmation here.

I am still tired. Why am I so tired? I guess it has been a long day. I am glad today was slow. I need to drop in to say hello to Eva Schmidt. I wish I would have called first. There are many phone calls I seem to refuse to make.

It is solitary here. Even so, I could still hear the train whistle in White Earth. That's cool."

Cemetery near the homestead

"9/12/00, Cemetery down the road in White Earth. Stayed in Stanley. My legs were scratched up badly and I decided a hot bath was in order. It is less windy today and therefore feels warmer. Very few clouds. Beautiful. There is the click of grasshoppers in the grass. A little rusty fellow was

sitting on my book when I suggested he might be happier someplace else.

This is the strangest cemetery I have ever visited. I had just finished reading Arnold's diary from 1932 (*Post Graduate Vagabonding*). I entered the small cemetery and I was familiar with 90% of its inhabitants. All of those people in Arnold's black book are here. Nearly all of them.

Ole Hansen lived to be 98! Carl Thompson lived to be 92. Selma Schmidt, Joe Hanson, Norsted, Novik, Harold Schmidt, Bendick, Bendt. There are all here. ALL!

For never ever having been here before, I was amazed at the familiarity that this visit could bring. In a way, I felt like I knew them. Wouldn't Arnold have felt strange about seeing them here? Perhaps he wouldn't have bothered. Selma Schmidt's grave is amongst a large bush. It is mostly hidden but I am glad that I saw it. Arnold thought of her as a kind woman. She fed him often enough.

I read through Arnold's excerpts from his summer at White Earth in 1932. Actually, he is quite insulting to many who now reside here. I guess he was kind of a jerk at times. You have to take his opinions with a grain of salt. A visit with Eva is warranted although I hesitate now about showing her Arnold's diary even though he does not disparage the Schmidt's. I will have to decide when I see her.

I have been interrupted by two black cows charging the fence and making a racket. I wonder if my presence by the cemetery bothers them. They are quietly nuzzling each other. Perhaps there is another interest now. Many little white moths are flitting over the grasses. Small, yellow flowers are growing down here. The grass is yellowing. Fall is very near here even though you wouldn't know it from the weather. I again feel like napping. What's the deal here anyway? I would like to do so but I wonder if the locals would get upset with somebody sleeping near the cemetery gate? There is a Gladys G. Heglund in the cemetery. I wonder if this is Gladys Dolan? Theory is that she stayed here to raise a family. It says 1908-1996. I would have thought that if this were her she would have been born closer to 1903-1904. I need to ask Eva."

Back at the homestead and coulee

"9/13/00, Minot. Taking out some time to do laundry and will check my email this morning. I did not call and see if Ella Bolen is still alive. Maybe tonight. I should've done it last night, but didn't get here until after 10:00.

I spent the afternoon yesterday in the coulee. I went to visit Eva Schmidt but she was going to a funeral so I decided to come back at 4:00. She is a sweet lady and I ended up spending 4 hours with her. She made me dinner and I helped her feed her 20-25 cats.

I talked to Gladys Dolan's daughter. Gladys passed away over 25 years ago!! More than just missed her.

In the coulee I walked down from the road where I thought the Schmidt land may have been.

I walked down into the trees going down into the valley. There was a lake down there. Although it was a bit stagnant. No fresh springs. Many, many deer down there. A couple of beaver dams, I believe. I think Arnold's hangout was to the SW of where I was but there is no real way to know.

My throat is definitely sore. Great! Motivation low. I am tempted to strike towards town. However, I must see Landa even though I know nothing about the place. So I guess I will head to Bottineau later. Then buzz there either Thursday or Friday.

I am embarrassed that I didn't make my calls, but then perhaps it's not as important as I think.

Eva was a sweet woman. I think she had a great fondness for Arnold. She said that Arnold often told her that he loved her and wanted to marry her. I gave her the journal (the copy). I think that she will enjoy it. She was packing to go to Alaska on the 14th. A cruise with some of her many buddies."

Skip ahead now to the present (2015)

White Earth is hardly the sleeping town that Sunny visited fifteen years earlier. White Earth currently finds itself sitting on a massive oil deposit, the Bakken Field. One would now see a scene of oil rigs, pumping stations, trucks and trains that run constantly all day to move the oil. White Earth can't keep up with the surging population of incoming oil workers. When Sunny visited in 2000, the population was 63. In 2013 the population was estimated to have risen to 500. This probably does not include all the people who live in cars, trucks and ramshackle trailers even in the frigid winters. Temporary restaurants and bars have been erected. At night White Earth has an otherworldly appearance, like an alien invasion with flames coming out of the ground, the light combining with the darkness. In 2013, a documentary film entitled *White Earth* was made by J. Christiansen Jensen, and it was nominated for an Academy Award. It is the White Earth oil experience as seen through the eyes of children. It is not always a positive thing. When the oil is gone, will White Earth again return to an almost deserted sleeping town?

Chapter Two: Minot, N.D.

After Sammy graduated from the White Earth High School in June 1922, she followed her principal's advice and decided to prepare for teaching rather than nursing, which she had considered. He said to her, "With your personality you belong in a school room."[4] She elected to attend the Normal School in Minot, North Dakota, to accomplish this goal.

Normal schools were the first colleges to train elementary-school teachers for teaching in public schools. Normal school education was an improvement from the former practice of assigning teaching responsibilities to the most deserving eighth-grade graduate—the system used when Sammy was attending the Hanson School in White Earth. The early normal schools usually had a two-year course. That later expanded to four years and the schools evolved into teachers' colleges.

---

[4] Doles, Lucy, <u>By Lucy Doles</u>, in *Racine Daily News*. 1931: Racine, Wisconsin.

It had become a Samuelson family tradition to attend the Normal School. Sammy's older sister Anna had graduated

MAIN BUILDING WITH FUTURE WEST WING.

from the school a year earlier and had become a teacher. Her brother Samuel was in the Advanced Curriculum when Sammy arrived in the fall of 1922. He later taught school for a short time, then became a doctor. Younger brother Arnold attended the University of Minnesota and graduated with a degree in journalism.

It was quite remarkable that all of these four children of poor, Norwegian immigrants attained degrees in higher education at that time. The parents were unable to help them financially, so each did this on their own. Tuition was free at the Normal School after paying a $5 registration fee. Students needed to buy textbooks, but used ones were available that could be later sold back to the school. Sammy supported herself by working in the school cafeteria. She probably lived in the Women's Dormitory, where room and board cost $18 a month.

LADIES' DORMITORY TO BE COMPLETED NOV. 15, 1923.

Besides her study and work, she found time to participate in school activities. She enjoyed outdoor sports, and excelled in musical and acting events at the school.

BOATING PARTY ON MOUSE RIVER NEAR THE SCHOOL.

Sammy's personality was described after her death by her friend Corrine Babcock, a fellow student at the Normal School: "Although she was a senior, and had taught school for two terms and I was a sophomore, our courses threw us together in several classes. She was exceptionally bright and always among the honor students. I never knew or heard of her going out with a boy, although she was beautiful with rich red hair, lovely coloring and fine features. It seemed to me that Hedvig, raised on a North Dakota farm, working her way by helping in a cafeteria, winning student honors, just didn't have time for such things. She was always frank about her finances. I remember that once I handed her a note in a class, asking her to go somewhere and she scribbled in one of my textbooks. 'I haven't the cash.' We knew each other well. I lived when not at school with an aunt in West Hope. Sammy taught six miles away from West Hope at Landa. Often we went home together on the same train for the weekends from Minot. Everyone who knew her loved her."[5] Marion Vrem said that they were classmates together in Minot. She talked about her beauty and popularity and her eagerness that others

---

[5] *Friend Recalls Trunk Murder Victim's Beauty, in San Francisco News,* October 23, 1931: San Francisco.

should escape the suffering of tuberculosis. She described Sammy as one of the best ice skaters at Minot and a splendid horsewoman. She said, "After graduation we wrote to each other frequently. I called her Sammy as all her friends did."[6]

Sammy made good use of her singing and acting abilities. On Jan. 31, 1924, Minot celebrated a Mid-Winter Festival at the Minot Normal School. As part of the festival, a play called "Chimes of Normandy" was presented. Hedvig played the role of Suzanne, one of the Village Maidens.

Sammy was chosen to participate as a member of the Glee Club. The yearbook shows a picture of the Glee Club members wearing wide-collared sweaters; Sammy appears to be wearing a tie. The yearbook states, "If a visitor, listening to the first Glee Club practice in October had been asked to define that 'concord of sweet sounds' he would probably have called it 'an attempt to express the emotions that are beyond speech.' However, Mr. Bland has proved himself worthy of much praise for his untiring efforts with his group of warblers, and now the girls might even be able to 'sooth the savage beast' if it weren't more ferocious than a lap-dog or a kitty. The Glee Club, one of the oldest organizations in the school, has advanced in long strides under the direction of Mr. Bland, in spite of the fact that he was handicapped by being new here." Sammy continued as a Glee Club Member throughout her standard course and advanced curriculum. She was listed as a soprano. The group practiced at 3:30 p.m. on

---

[6] *Trunk Victims Friend is Found, in Sam Francisco News.* October 22, 1931: San Francisco.

Wednesdays. In the yearbook, it was said, "Under the competent direction of Mr. Bland, the Girls' Glee Club has progressed greatly. Much local recognition has been accorded to them. On several occasions the assembly has been entertained by the 'Wonderful Warblers.'" Sammy participated in the Graduation exercises (The Senior Sermon) on June 8, 1924. She performed in a sextet that sang "I Will Exalt Thee." The *Magician*, the school's year book from that year,

shows Sammy as an elementary senior student. Next to her picture is the quote, "When she has left she will leave a place no one can fill." The following year, 1925, Sammy was listed in the *Magician* as an advanced senior, and the quote now was, "How music, that stirs all one's devout emotions, blends everything into harmony." In her picture, Sammy is wearing the black shirt with the ermine collar that was later printed in newspapers after her death. The yearbook lists her as being a member of the Mecca for Pep, Glee Club, the Home Economics Club and the YWCA. Sammy was described as "a young woman of pleasing presence, happy disposition and most excellent character." The graduation ceremony when Sammy graduated from the advanced curriculum course for teachers was held on July 24, 1925, in the school gymnasium. The music included "Send out Thy Light," "Triumph Polka," and "Old Sweet Song." President George A. McFarland presided and Miss Minnie J. Nielson, State Superintendent of Public Instruction, gave the address and conferred the diplomas. In the summer of 1925, Sammy attended summer courses. The school

put on the Gilbert and Sullivan opera *The Mikado* on July 23. Daily rehearsals were during the previous month. Sammy played one of the lead parts, Yum-Yum. Newspaper reports, "Mr. Trotter has a voice of pleasing quality, and his solos, and duets with Yum-Yum were among the entertaining features of the evening. Miss Hedvig Samuelson was a delectable Yum-Yum, having vivacity and a small, but sweet voice."[7] The paper gave the description of quaint maids in kimonos, with chrysanthemums in their hair, accompanying their mincing steps, with much fluttering of fans, flitting about the stage during the performance. More than 70 people were involved in the production.

---

[7] *"Students of College Register Decided Hit in Delightful Mikado,* in *Minot Daily News,* July 24, 1925: Minot, ND. 10

Another one of Sammy's school mates says of her, "I remember her standing in the curve of the grand piano long after classes were over, singing difficult passages again and again for the music director, an exceptionally irritable and temperamental man. But Sammy could get along with him, and he swore by her. She got along with everybody in the entire school, faculty and students alike. There was probably no better liked girl in the college. She was always smiling and always sincere. I never remember her saying an unkind or a catty thing about anyone, no matter what the provocation. She was extremely attractive, rather than beautiful by the accepted standards. Her lovely soprano voice immediately took her to the front in the school's and the city's amateur music circles." She also remembers her rehearsing "One Fine Day" from Madame Butterfly, wearing the same dress she wore for her school picture. She said that they wore their skirts long that year and Sammy's frock of black velvet with a band of ermine at the neck stunningly contrasted with her Norse fairness and her queer greenish-grey-eyes."[8] Sammy started the advanced curriculum in the summer of 1925. Her Landa, North Dakota, teaching assignment, it seems, was part of a practice teaching experience that she began the following fall.

Sunny visits Minot

Sunny visited Minot many times searching for traces of Sammy. She left few written accounts of these visits. However, she particularly liked visiting Roosevelt (Riverside) Park. After much study, she concluded that some previously unidentified photos in her family's album were

---

[8] Doles, Lucy, *By Lucy Doles*, in *Racine Daily News*, 1931: Racine, Wisconsin 1, 7

from this place. There is a photo of Sammy skating near a bridge

overpass. She is with an unidentified friend. First thinking that this was from Alaska, Sunny

later concluded that this was at the Mouse River near Minot after locating a postcard showing such a bridge in Minot. A park pavilion can also be seen in the background. This solved the mystery of the location of three other photos as well. Sammy and her friend

are dressed in heavy winter coats in the three pictures, which were obviously all taken the same day. In one picture, they are sitting near the park pavilion. In a second, they are near a rabbit hutch, which could be part of the zoo in the park. In the third picture, they on a stone fountain in the park. Her friend, not identified, could have been a classmate from Minot or a friend from her home in White Earth.

Sunny also found a picture that puzzled her. It depicts Sammy with four race car drivers on July 5 of an undetermined year. Sunny wondered if it had been taken at a race track near Minot. She eventually decided that it was. Sunny came to that conclusion a month

before her own death when she heard the race track sounds from her motel room while visiting Minot for the last

time in June 2014. She thought it was fun to get such a blaring clue telling her to pay attention to something. They have had races at the Minot Fairgrounds since 1921. Sammy could have been there in July 1930, or perhaps in 1925 or 1926.

CHAPTER THREE: LANDA, N.D.

SAMMY'S FIRST TEACHING JOB WAS at Landa, North Dakota, in the fall of 1925. She taught there throughout the school year. This may have been in conjunction with student practice teaching through the Minot Normal School. Landa is a small town in Bottineau County, about seven miles south of the Canadian border. It was founded by Norwegian immigrants in 1904, a year after the Great Northern Railway extended its way westward. The town's population was about 140 in 1930. At that time it had a bank, a hardware store, a lumberyard, a hotel, several churches, a school and other establishments.

Sammy boarded with the Louis Bogstie family in Landa most of the time during that year. This was a Norwegian family consisting of Louis, his wife Clara and their

three children, ages 11, 9 and 3. Louis was a grain buyer for the grain elevator in town. A family named Hagen also boarded other teachers and various others staying in town. Sammy was romantically interested in the 28-year-old son, Howard Hagen, who worked for his father. He helped her pack up after her school term ended in the summer of 1926 and helped her ship her trunk home to White Earth. From his letters to her, it was a sad occasion for him when Sammy left town. They corresponded regularly for about five years. Some of his letters were later made public and showed affection between them. When Sammy was in Phoenix, she received word that Howard had married and had become a father. Some of her diary entries showed she was disappointed at hearing the news.

Sunny visits Landa

Sunny stopped by Landa on Sept. 13, 2000, which then had a population of 28 people. Sunny writes in a travel diary, "The cats are the loudest thing here. This place is so small they have an outdoor post office. However, at one time this town supported two white stereotypical churches, and a medium sized school I believe. The school seems fairly new (for Sammy). However, it now looks like it has been converted to an auto shop. (The back is open and a bunch of guys are standing around back there. A radio is playing). The lacy curtains still hangs in the front. I am sitting at the bottom of a rusty slide in a park (or ex-school yard). There is a small hump closer to the deserted church. I am thinking a school might have been there. Or very possibly there was another school where the other (50's style?) school is. That building is the newest structure here. There is an old abandoned house adjacent to the park. It is open. Everything is in there for the most part too. Most of the playground equipment is broken. I saw one white cat and one black cat. Contrast. The mosquitos are furiously hungry. I guess I will stop at the cemetery and let this town continue to sleep."

CHAPTER FOUR: WHITEHALL, MT

SAMMY ARRIVED IN WHITEHALL in August 1926 for her second teaching assignment. Whitehall is a town in southwestern Montana in Jefferson County. There was record enrollment in the Whitehall Schools that fall. Sammy was one of four new teachers, and she taught second grade. Her first residence was at the "Sugar Hotel"—a dormitory created by repurposing a sugar beet factory boarding house. Groups of high school students from rural areas lived there along with several of the teachers. In the fall of 1926, 27 teachers and students

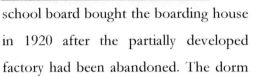

were living at the dormitory. Perhaps Sammy served as a supervisor or house mother to the students.

The school board bought the boarding house in 1920 after the partially developed factory had been abandoned. The dorm

was east of the lonely unused smokestack of the forgotten sugar factory. It sat on five acres of land southeast of the school and near a pond which was a popular ice skating place. The dorm, which was torn down after the property was sold in 1929, was so remote that in December 1926, when the weather was rainy, drivers were warned not to drive to the dorm area unless they were willing to risk getting stuck in the mud. Mr. Houx, the dorm director, built a boardwalk from the dorm porch to the road to ease access across the mud.

The dorm was a lively place for the students and teachers. They enjoyed many social activities while Sammy lived there during her first school year. The Jefferson Valley News recorded the activities of the dorm each week in the dormitory notes.

The dorm sponsored several dances that first year. From a dance on October 15, residents raised enough money to purchase a pool table. The table got a lot of use. A rule was made that nobody was to play pool after 2:30 in the morning. Later it was recorded that some boys were up playing pool until after 4:30. So much the rule! In December, residents purchased a Victrola for the dorm. It was said to be heard "all of the day and night." For Christmas, Santa Claus brought the first radio to the dorm. The residents joked that the most frequent station received was S-T-A-T-I-C. However, from time to time other stations came in. To celebrate the coming of spring, Elwood Lewis took out his saxophone and played "Home Sweet Home" over and over. Many threatened to move out.

On Oct. 15, 1926, the teachers and students at the dorm trekked to Morrison's Cave. The tour for the teachers and students on this Sunday was not led by Morrison, but by a homesteader in the area, Howard Woodward.

They left the dorm at 10:00 in the morning and returned that evening. In early days, a visit to this cave (now called Louis and Clark Caverns and located near Three Fork) was an all-day activity. One had to climb the mountain from the Jefferson River 1,500 feet up the cliff to the opening of the cave. When the cave had first been discovered, visitors had to lower themselves by rope into the opening. But by the time the dorm residents visited, Morrison had constructed a wooden spiral staircase into the cave. The staircase was unsteady, swaying 3-4 feet in either direction. The first stage of the descent brought visitors down 300 feet. Then visitors, aided by lanterns or candles, had to crawl on all fours into the first chamber, called "Caskets of the Gods" because of formations in that room that resembled caskets. The party then moved into a larger chamber called the "Cathedral Room." Today, there is still a small clear pool in this area that was used in the Twenties as a refreshment stop and later a wishing well. The copper from the coins has turned the water slightly green. After visiting this area, Sammy and her friends would have returned to the stairs and walked down 300 more steps. There they would have entered the "Organ Room," where

STAIRWAY TO THE GREAT MORRISON CAVE.
WHITEHALL, MONTANA

the stalactites are in the shape of a pipe organ. Back then visitors did not hesitate to strike the stalactites to produce various tones.

Near the bottom of the cave, the dorm residents would have stopped for a lunch break near the brown waterfall. Then they would have climbed the 600 steps to the open air and made their way down the mountain.

Sammy's second-graders studied various subjects, and holiday activities at Thanksgiving, Halloween and Christmas were incorporated into their work. For instance, they would cut pumpkins, turkeys or Santa Claus figures out of paper, use them in artwork and write about them. They learned about Eskimos and their culture and tried to build an igloo. They were glad they didn't have to eat

JOURNEY TO HEALTH LAND

ADDRESS

III

HIAWATHA'S CHICKENS

Then the little Hiawatha
Learned of every bird its language,
Learned their names and all their secrets,
How they built their nests in Summer,
Where they hid themselves in Winter,
Talked with them whene'er he met them,
Called them "Hiawatha's Chickens."

Henry Wadsworth Longfellow.

an Eskimo diet. They studied Indians and read Henry Wadsworth Longfellow's poem *Song of Hiawatha*, which included a section called "Hiawatha's Chickens." They were also taught health and hygiene and read a book called *A Journey to Health Land*. They learned music, also, and were taught to identify orchestral instruments and the tones they made. The children were involved in putting on plays and entering artistic contests organized by their teachers. The teachers took turns supervising the lunch rooms, the study halls, and playground. In the winter after a good snow, the children enjoyed playing "Fox and Geese," a game in which the Fox, who was it, would chase the others, the Geese, around a pie-shaped area in the snow.

In Whitehall, Sammy shared her singing and acting talents as she had done at Minot. At a school assembly on Nov. 24, 1926, she sang a vocal solo called "Out of the Dust." In December of 1926 the teachers put on a play called *Second Childhood*. The play was by Zellah Covington. Sammy played Sylvia Relgea. The character Sylvia is the daughter of Professor Frederick Relgea, who thinks he has discovered the elixir of youth. His young assistant Philip Stanton wants to marry Sylvia, but so does General Henry Burbeck, an elderly man. The professor is going to lose his house and needs to borrow $10,000 from the General. Philip and the Professor think that the General has drunk a whole bottle of the elixir when a baby is left at the house by a Spanish woman. Sylvia is angry at Phil and decides to marry the General. Meanwhile, another baby is left at the house and Philip and the Professor think it's Sylvia. Sylvia and the General arrive back at the house ready to be married, but the Professor and Philip think they are ghosts since they are dressed in white. Of course, everything works out in the end. Admission to the performance was 50 cents.

Christmas was a big event celebrated in the school. A large Christmas tree was delivered for the Christmas program in 1926. Santa Claus, assisted by the boy scouts, made an appearance with 400 or 500 sacks of sweets and fruit. The Christmas program started at 8 p.m. The first- and second-graders presented the play *The Toy Shop*. This program was directed by Ella Bolen, assisted by Sammy. Other parts of the program included tableaus and Christmas carols led by the third graders. The fourth-, fifth- and sixth-graders presented an operetta called *The Fairy Conspiracy*. Marian Huntley, sister of Chet Huntley, who would later become a celebrated newscaster, played the part of Beauty.

The school experienced some trying events during these years. Scarlet fever was a problem in the dorm in 1926. All of the residents of the dorm were given several series of inoculations. Some students were sent away and quarantined. School had to be canceled on Nov. 15, 1926, because the furnace went out. Classes had to be moved to the gymnasium in the high school for several weeks while the furnace was being repaired, and school was chaotic. Things didn't get better the

following year. On May 19, 1927, the Whitehall High School burned down. At times, there were reports that someone was poisoning dogs in Whitehall.

However, life was not all trouble and worry. The teachers were included in the life of the larger community and took part in many enjoyable activities. Parties and dinners were hosted by the elite members of Whitehall, and the teachers were among those invited. Residents liked to play the popular card game Five Hundred, with lunch served afterward. On one of these occasions, the game winners were given prizes of a Shari compact in pink satin for the woman and a utility set for the man. The consolation prize was a rubber cap for the lady and a rubber cigar for the man. For this game, the lunch served afterward featured creamed chicken and noodles, potato chips, pickles, cheese sandwiches, orange and devil's food cake and coffee.

Sammy went to a Halloween party on Oct. 25, 1926, and her friend Ella Bolen got the low score in Five Hundred. After cards, the guests were ushered into a room of spooks and goops, where they were presented with favors and fortunes.

Mrs. Lot Borden, a prominent member of the community and owner of the Modern Hotel, gave many dinner parties for special events. On Nov. 17, 1927, she held such a party in honor of Sammy's twenty-fourth birthday at the restaurant in the hotel. The table was decorated with yellow chrysanthemums with place cards and nut cups in matching color. Sammy received many beautiful gifts.

Most of the female teachers were part of the Whitehall Women's Club, which met regularly. On Feb. 14, 1928, the meeting was at the Borden Block a prominent area of town owned by Lot and Hilda Borden which at one time included a two hotels, a saloon and billiard room, a dining hall as well as a dance hall. The attendees arrived in old fashioned costumes dating from 1810 to 1920. After the meeting and a

program and musical entertainment, those in costume put on a style show and gave the history and date of their creation. Sammy wore a heavily embroidered nightgown and nightcap in a style popular a century and a half before. Mrs. Packard, the doctor's wife, read a few notes on etiquette taken from a manual written ninety years before. Then Mrs. Harbison followed with a few extracts from Emily Post's new book on etiquette. Childhood photos of some of ladies in attendance were shown around and everyone guessed who they were. Lunch was then served. A Mrs. Pace was supposed to serve the meal but was ill, so those in costume called upon her afterward so she would not miss the fun.

This picture is from Montana but Sammy's friend is unknown. Is this Ella Bolen or Jessica Kramer?

Most of the teachers left Whitehall for the holidays. Since Sammy was far from her family in White Earth, North Dakota, she was invited both years she was there to spend the holidays with a friend, Jessica Kramer (later Williams). They traveled to Elk Basin on the border between Wyoming and Montana, northeast of Cody. They stopped in Bozeman on the way back. After Sammy's death, Jessica Williams said of her: "When we were at Whitehall, Sammy was almost like a sister to me. I've thought all day of the terrible affair, but can't figure out any reason for it"..."Everyone loved her so well. I can't understand why such a girl as Sammy had to be mixed up in a thing like this. She was very attractive and quiet until you knew her quite well."[9]

In February 1927, Sammy became ill with pneumonia so severe that a new teacher had to replace her for six weeks. She was treated by the Whitehall doctor, Dr. Packard. A Mrs. Vest provided nursing care. Mrs. Vest was the Aunt Cela that Chet Huntley referred to in a piece about Sammy in his book, *The Generous Years* (quoted below). Chet Huntley's sister Peggy was one of Sammy's students, not Marian as Chet Huntley had stated. Sammy recovered sufficiently from her bout with pneumonia to sign a contract to teach the following year (1927-1928). This included 180 days of actual teaching, not including holidays or recesses. She was to be paid $1,150 in ten equal installments. The contract stated if Sammy was absent or ill, she would receive 50 percent of her salary for up to 20 days. After 20 days, Whitehall was not obliged to pay her.

---

[9] *Teacher Tells of her Friendship*, in *Montana Standard*. October 21, 1931: Butte, Montana, 2.

Sammy visited Landa, probably to visit with Howard Hagen, during the summer of 1927 and spent time with her family in White Earth. She returned to teach her second year in Whitehall and probably lived at the Palm Hotel, which was connected to the Modern Hotel run by Mrs. Lot Borden on the Borden Block. Perhaps this was quieter than living in the dormitory, or perhaps not with the dance hall, billiards, a tavern and dining room associated with it.

Chet Huntley wrote the following about Sammy in his book, *The Generous Years*:

The majority of the teachers in the Whitehall primary and secondary schools boarded and roomed at the Palm Hotel or at a dormitory managed by the school board and located in what had been planned as the living quarters for the employees of the sugar factory. The sugar company had halted its construction halfway through the project, leaving a tall smokestack, a row of executive houses and the dormitory. Frequently these "homeless" teachers were guests in our home for one of Mother's heralded dinners. Among these appreciative guests was Marian's teacher, Miss Samuelson.

Freshly out of teachers' college in North Dakota, Hedvig Samuelson was a singular girl: decidedly attractive, bright, and finely balanced between gay aggressiveness and reserved shyness. Sammy Samuelson was one of the very rare young teachers in that small community who managed the no mean feat of avoiding local gossip.

As I recall, it was during the second year of her tenure in the Whitehall school system that Sammy was taken ill with a severe attack of pneumonia. Aunt Cela, who was visiting us at the time, helped nurse her back to health, and she returned to the classroom for the spring months. On her doctor's advice, however, Sammy took a position for the following year in the primary school in Juneau, Alaska. From correspondence with some of the townspeople we then learned that she had contracted a mild case of tuberculosis and was going to spend some time in Phoenix, Arizona. With what shock and dismay, about three years later, we saw Sammy's name and photograph on the front pages, frequently above lurid captions. From all over the nation friends sent the newspaper clippings. Sammy was a victim in the incredible Winnie Ruth Judd case, her dismembered body found in a trunk in the Los Angeles railroad station. A number of newspapers reprinted a bloodstained photograph taken from the trunk, and captioned it: HEDVIG SAMUELSON AND UNIDENTIFIED BOYFRIEND. It was a snapshot of Sammy and me standing on our front porch.[10]

Sunny visits Whitehall

Again retracing Sammy's travels, Sunny visited Whitehall on Sept. 4, 2000. The town population was now 1,044 people, probably down considerably from 1928. The evening she arrived, Sunny instinctively made her way down the road to a lone smokestack, which stood on the site of an old auto junkyard with a pole barn. There was a tiny cement foundation there, perhaps 100 feet square. Weeds grew thickly. There had been no structure on the foundation for many, many years. The site was littered with burned green linoleum and an old mattress frame. Sunny speculated that this was the site of the unfinished sugar factory, or possibly of the dorm Sammy lived in. She felt close to it.

There was another, smaller, foundation to the west, and a red brick structure to the east. Sunny suspected that those may have been dormitories. There was an old brick house across the way. Somebody still lived there.

---

[10] Huntley, Chet, *The Generous Years*, 1968. 191-192

At the house, some older men had gathered. Sunny heard them say 1926, North Dakota, and school teacher. Her ears perked up. She wondered if one of the guys was Roy Milligern, who she was to meet later.

Sunny visited the Jefferson Valley Museum, found it overwhelming, but of little value to her. At the museum, she met with Margaret Scott. Margaret and Howard, the boy Margaret would later marry, had been taught by Sammy as second-grade students. Margaret said Sammy had been absent often one year and was replaced during those periods by a substitute teacher. No doubt this had been her second year of teaching, when she contracted pneumonia. Margaret recalled that Sammy was a nice teacher but didn't remember anything else about her, except that she was murdered. Sunny spoke with Roy Milligern who was in charge of the museum. He called around looking for others who might have known Sammy, but most of them only knew her as the one who had been killed. For the size of the town, the museum was impressive. Roy said he had to rescue some of the things displayed there from the dump. Sunny found out that the dormitory for the school was east of the town. It had 32 sleeping rooms in 1930. The dormitory had been bought from the owners of the abandoned sugar factory for $6,500. In the building's first year of operation as a dorm, it housed 45 students and nine faculty members, each paying $18 a month. It had been torn down in April 1933 after a fire. The "Sugar Hotel" had a day area, kitchen, shower and double baths, and a large laundry. People went to the Pipestone Hot Springs to swim and take medicinal and vapor baths. This is about five miles west of the town. Dr. Packard arrived in 1902. He had gotten his degree in medicine so he could remain in school longer to play football. He was also mayor from 1923 to 1927. He was a chunky guy who served the town of Whitehall for more than 40 years.

Sunny did not feel Sammy's presence here. Sunny felt she may have been too concerned about writing. She wasn't sure. She felt something the first evening as she walked down Sugar Beet Row, but only a feeling. She felt perhaps it was only anticipation. Whether Sammy lived there or not, she had walked there many times, Sunny felt sure of that.

Sunny did find a local paper called the *Jefferson Valley News*. She thought she could go through several years of this paper from 1926 on, in Helena. She also felt the pull to move on. However, she felt she needed to know Whitehall better before she did. Rain was forecast but had held off. Though the temperature was 80 degrees and it was sunny where she was, the sky in the west was dark. She felt she should walk. She wondered where people hiked here. Roy didn't know. She drove down Division Thoroughfare and ended up at the Jefferson River. She thought Sammy must have walked there. Most of the land now seemed private and fenced. She thought she would drive over to the hot springs at Pipestone, although she had heard it was just private land now. Roy said everybody went over there to swim, bathe, and to have facials. She thought about driving over and looking around. She decided to first drive to Helena and return to the town afterward. She stayed overnight in Helena, and on September 9, she was able to review the *Jefferson Valley News*, where she found out much of the information about Sammy's time in Whitehall related above. On her way back toward Whitehall, she drove over the Continental Divide and saw spire-like rocks. The rocks were spooky, almost mystical. She remembered a picture of a lake with spire-like rocks that she had seen

in her family's photo collection. She had thought that depicted a scene in Alaska, but now she began to think that perhaps she was near this lake. When she saw a sign that said Delmoe Lake was 11 miles away down a really bad road she decided to explore. But when she got to the lake, there were very few rocks, none of them spire-like.

Sunny listed things she wanted to remember about Whitehall. She was interested in the Borden Block since Sammy probably lived at the Palm Hotel, part of the complex owned by the Bordens. She knew Sammy had been a friend of Hilda Borden, who hosted her twenty-fourth birthday in the dining room of her restaurant. The hotel she visited was now called the Borden Hotel. She wanted to remember the wallpaper at Borden's — round raised-print wallpaper, the staircase in the middle room going up to the rooms, bare beechwood walls now painted white and a sign that said Borden's in the center room. A picture of Mrs. Lot "Hilda" Borden hanging above the cash register. The area was now referred to as Borden's Corner but was called the Borden's Block in the papers. In a corner of the center room there was a step that said Borden's Corner.

Since Sunny visited Borden's Corner, none of the things she wanted to remember are still there. A gas explosion caused a fire that destroyed the building in 2009. However, in 2013 the area underwent a $1.5

million renovation and is now operating as a historical hotel. It is Whitehall's only historically registered building. The hotel includes some retail space on the street level with some apartments on the second floor. However, the raised- print wallpaper, the original staircase and the Borden signs were probably all destroyed.

Sunny had visited the Lewis and Clark Caverns State Park, previously known as Morrison's Cave, on September 7 on her way to Yellowstone. She writes in her diary: "This is a year to the date that I went to Alaska last year. Has my attitude changed? I have not experienced Sammy's presence yet. Sammy visited here on 10/17/26. Five years before her death. In those days, visiting Morrison's Cave was not for the faint of heart. It still isn't but it's a lot easier now. In the old days they need to travel there by the train or by river. Then they needed to walk down and then walk back out. Now, they have built another entrance. Seems (it would have been) more exciting in the old times with lanterns and candles instead of electric lights."

CHAPTER FIVE: YELLOWSTONE

SAMMY SPENT THE SUMMER OF 1928 at Yellowstone National Park. The park is located primarily in Wyoming, though it extends into Montana and Idaho. She left Whitehall on June 3, 1928, for Yellowstone. Several teachers from Whitehall planned to be employed there during the park season. The official opening date was not until June 15. Sammy may have motored to the park with them or she may have taken the train. There is a report that she worked in a curio shop there along with an Inez Westerdall.[11] The park was not too far from Whitehall, where Sammy had worked that school year.

Sunny visited Yellowstone National Park

Sunny visited Yellowstone on Sept. 8, 2000, to try to find traces that Sammy had been there, and recorded her trip in her travel diary. She stopped in Bozeman, Montana, but found little of interest there except the iced mocha. She entered the park at the north entrance and hiked around in the hot sulfur springs area, enjoying the white deposits, the

---

[11] *Mother explains listing of girl's name by victim*, in *Los Angeles Evening Herald*, October 22, 1931: Los Angeles, 11.

steam and smells. She looked through a library at the park but didn't find any signs of Sammy having been there. She researched newspaper articles and found interesting material, but no trace of Sammy.

She went over to Norris to see a geyser she called the "unfaithful geyser." A crowd had assembled, so she waited too. It had erupted at 10:30 a.m. and was expected to erupt again in 35-75 minutes but was about 100 minutes overdue. Three work chums traveling together from California had been waiting for over an hour. Sunny found them to be funny. One younger guy was freezing, there was an old retired guy and a guy in shorts with a T-shirt. She could see goose bumps on his legs. She chatted with them for half an hour until a small eruption finally occurred. It was hard to see since the steam overcame it for the most part. They all oohed and awed and made sexual types of comments about its inadequacy which she found to be pretty funny. She actually liked the smell of the sulfur. She decided to go to Old Faithful geyser the next day.

She felt safe camping near there for the night. The weather was great but the wind was so strong. She had to buy rope to tie the rocks down at the tent corners. The arrangement didn't look fashionable, but it would keep the tent from going anywhere. The weather was perfect at first, but then a heavy black cloud approached from the north – very black. The moon shone brightly in the clear south sky. She decided making a fire was too much work and referred to herself as a "lazy ass!" She decided that when she couldn't see anymore out there she would go to sleep. She was sickened by her survival skills. "To watch me tie down the tent must have been a riot! What a klutz. Well, it's past dark now and I am cold. I plan to climb into the union suit and pray that the dark cloud to the north doesn't plan to bring rain!"

And oh what a night!

"I retired about 8:30 but didn't sleep much. I was plenty warm with the flowered union suit inside the sleeping bag. I had nervous dreams. At one point during the night I was awakened by what I thought were screams of a woman. It sounded like it was on the hill a ways out. It continued. I decided if it were a woman there would be words. Either that or somebody was playing a rude joke. However, it actually sounded like a woman screaming into a funnel or horn. Very bizarre. This went on intermittently. Later, it was like it was next to the tent! It no longer sounded like a woman screaming but either a type of animal cry or a leader calling its followers. Then, thunder everywhere. It was upon me! I could hear the thundering hooves, right on top of me! Or, so it seemed! I stayed hidden in the sleeping bag, praying I wouldn't be trampled by the stampede. I assumed it wasn't as close as I had thought. (Like right on top of me). However, in the morning there were fresh hoof marks on both sides of the tent within two feet. I really was in the midst of a stampede! Then when the herd passed (Elk I presume), it started to rain! The tent sagged. I was surprised not to be soaked. However, the tent sagged almost to my hips which nearly touched it when I laid on my side. It was very difficult to get dressed and packed while laying on my back. When I arose, snow was falling in small pellets. Even so, I managed to lie there for 12 hours! I am happy the sun came out although it is cold! I am happy I camped and have never been under the sound of thundering hooves before. Wild! I don't know if I have the courage to try it again tonight. I stopped bathing and eating for the most part. Is this degenerating? I just haven't wanted to eat in days. I made myself drink the milk I brought for cereal."

Sunny drove over to Old Faithful and bought some Minestrone and rice and vegetables at the Old Faithful Dining Hall. A huge crowd had assembled by the geyser, which started to spew off first just 3-4 feet and then was calm. The crowd was calm and quiet as they waited. It was bigger than the other geyser that Sunny had seen the day before but she did not find it as much fun. "Perhaps the unknown of the other after examination and guesswork was more interesting. The crowd was more jovial too. The crowd here was silent for the most part. Perhaps more spontaneity is more interesting than the 'Old Faithful.' At least in my book."

"Now for a decision. Camp again, or work my way back towards Billings? The weather was clear, I should have camped. I certainly should not have driven like I did. I assumed the NW entrance would have been like the north entrance (fairly big down near the entrance, flat drive, about 70-75 mph to the highway). The speed limit was about

25 for miles and miles. I went up for about 20 miles. The sun was setting. I actually was ready to stop driving around along the park, but I thought it was in my best interest to keep driving while there was still light. I decided that I would park once it got dark but try to make it in one piece to Red Lodge if possible. At the top it was pretty well dark, but there was so much wind and snow I was afraid to stop. I was so tired that I should have stopped 2 hours earlier. I was short of gas! I put the car in neutral and coasted 20 miles downhill. I used the brake very little. It was so windy up there that I did need to use the brake to go downhill at times. I pretty much decided that I would be spending the night up there. Somehow I coasted into Red Lodge where there was some serious parties going on and hardly any place to stay. I didn't feel like spending $50 for a smoky room so I made the unwise decision to drive to Billings after gassing up. It was a flat easy drive, but I was worried about deer and drunks. Somehow, I made it safely to Billings."

Chapter Six: Alert Bay, B.C.

Sammy apparently visited Alert Bay on Cormorant Island in British Columbia sometime between 1928 and 1930. An old family album contains photos of totem poles that she took, but she left no clue as to their identity or location. Sunny was able to

determine that the photos were taken in Alert Bay. She surmised that

Sammy passed through here while traveling north from Vancouver, B.C., to Juneau, Alaska, where she taught school. Sunny knew Sammy had come through Vancouver on a ship, the *Princess Charlotte*, at least twice. Her adventurous spirit must have

caused her to stop at Alert Bay. Sammy probably traveled to the island by ferry from Port McNeill on Vancouver Island. This picture was in the family album and seems to be a ferry that Sammy could have taken to Alert Bay. In 2000, Sunny took a ferry, following Sammy's trail. As it turned out, Sunny, while visiting Alert Bay, was able to see more relics of the Nimkish people than Sammy did. Sammy would not have been able to view the masks used in potlatch ceremonies by the Nimkish. They had been confiscated in 1921 by the Canadian government as part of an effort by white Christians to assimilate the indigenous people into the dominant culture. By the time Sunny visited, an agreement had been reached and some of the masks and relics had been returned to the Nimkish. She viewed them in the new U'mista Cultural Centre. The two cultures now exist side by side on the island but retain their separate identities.

Sunny wrote about her visit to Alert Bay in the following piece.

Death of a Thunderbird

I know nothing.

But there are cycles.

There are circles.

There are connections.

I am disappointed. I approach the Nimkish burial ground for the first time. Dilapidated grave totems stand lonely on the hill. They are rotting and falling over from neglect. Others seem vandalized. I wonder why the totems have not been cared for. I see a wooden eagle on the top of a pole that is about to fall off. It leans decisively to the left. Most of the thunderbirds are now wingless. Many have a stick protruding from one of its sides where a wing once was. Others seem amputated as if the wings were torn off. Now they appear as powerless birds, defeated. No sign of either of the totems that I drove to Alert Bay to see; the dual mighty thunderbirds and the grave marker of Sisooth, the two-headed snake.

I make my way down the road, past the ferry. This becomes the reservation. Even in 2000, the island seems divided, the native half and the white half. Garbage lines the beach. A broken down pier bares a sign that says, "Do not drive on the pier." I laugh. One look at that pier would dissuade any person from even considering walking there, let alone driving on it. On either side, the pier leans precariously at 45-degree angles. Just when it looks like it is going to fall, it shifts and leans viciously the other way. Broken down boats with whole sides missing are moored in the muck on the beach. Certainly, they were not going anywhere-ever. I see a canoe with Sisooth on the side. The canoe is white and new. Sisooth, the two-headed snake, arches across the canoe and his reflection appears on the water. The well maintained canoe contrasts sorely with the gray day and the broken down boats. Seaweed and an old rope lie on the beach next to the murky water. A cruise ship passes.

I approach the old school and the new cultural center. A lone wingless thunderbird faithfully stands guard at the entrance to the drive. A stick stands out on its side at a 90-degree angle where his wing once was. A hollow well is all that is left of his beak. The grizzly bear that he is standing on has lost his teeth. The bear's nose is absent. This thunderbird along with the bear is no longer a fierce protector. His partner was missing. Only a solitary post, affixed to a cement slab is left.

I study the picture Sammy, my great aunt, had taken in 1928 or 1930. Two thunderbirds protected the door of the chief. Even in those days, the house next door had boarded up windows. The dual thunderbirds were immaculate and contrasted severely with the dilapidated shack. Their arched wingspan matched their height. A wooden walkway appears in the forefront of the picture. These birds were once fierce protectors. The talons latched tightly to the bear's head. The bear's fangs appear sharp.

I wonder why Sammy had come here at all. Boats traveling to Juneau, Alaska, where she taught school, passed through here on the way north from Vancouver. I knew that she had

traveled through Vancouver on the *Princess Charlotte* at least twice. I had two pictures to guide me. I retraced their origin and ended up on this island, on this reservation, only to find myself staring up at a rotting, amputated thunderbird. He seemed powerless and defeated.

I bought a postcard of the thunderbirds in a better day. The post card stated that the thunderbird is the noble and omnipotent ruler of the skies and master over the elements. Light rain misted down. I think that this thunderbird is clearly losing the battle with the elements.

Porous rotten hole-like sores appear all over his body. What happened to his partner?

An unassuming native man appears behind me. I do not notice him at first. He is wearing a gray and black flannel shirt, baseball cap, and jeans. He wears his hair short. He says, "These were nice thunderbirds. Maybe somebody will remake them someday."

I ask, "Do people still make these?"

He replies, "Some do. I make the knife blades for everybody in the tribe. It keeps me pretty busy. It is not our way to repair the poles. When one falls, we build a new one. An erected pole has served its purpose. The other bird is in the campground."

"In the campground?" I ask.

He replies, "It fell off the pole. Usually, we would leave it where it fell. However, it was in the road, in the way. It blocked the drive up to the school. So, we put it back in the campground."

"Where is the campground?"

"Oh, it's up the road past the Big House on the other side of the island," he explains. Then, he is gone as quickly as he arrived. I take a few pictures of the remaining thunderbird and his partner, the vacant pole. Sammy had seen these door posts through different eyes, I am sure. Had she sent me here with the old photographs to witness their demise?

I walk up the drive past the old school. The residential school was built in 1929 to teach the Indian children. Now it is the tribal office, a new purpose for an old building. The school appears to have been red brick, but was painted white years ago. The white paint is peeling off to reveal the red brick again.

I enter the new U'mista Cultural Centre. A women immediately places me in a room alone to watch a video about the museum collection. I learn that the Canadian government outlawed the potlatch in 1895, one of the tribe's ceremonies. The natives continued to celebrate the potlatch in secret anyway. In 1921, many were arrested in Alert Bay while participating in this ceremony. The white man took their masks and other items and scattered them all over North America. They locked them away, put them behind glass, and hid them away. The tribe reached an agreement with the Canadian government in the late seventies. They would return the items and bring them back to Alert Bay. In exchange, the tribe would build a museum to house and display these items permanently. The collection returned in 1980, with much celebration by the tribe. They celebrated the Potlatch.

In earlier days people were taken captive by raiding parties. When they returned to their homes, either through payment or by a retaliating raid, they were said to have U'mista. These treasures have a U'mista of their own. They returned to alert Bay after almost 60 years. The masks are openly displayed. They returned home.

Was I experiencing U'mista? Certainly, I nor my Norwegian relatives ever belonged in this place. And yet, Sammy at least passed through Alert Bay in 1928 or 1930. The pictures were all that I knew of this trip. There were no written account or family stories. Only two pictures in the family albums recorded this story. She must have sent these pictures home to North Dakota in a letter.

I feel somehow that I had returned to Alert Bay even though I had never been there before. After all, she was my grandfather's adventurous sister. Weren't some of her genes recycled and reused in me? I feel as though I were revisiting again after 70 years. Part of me had been there before. I am returning, completing a cycle. The masks were taken before Sammy arrived here. Now they have returned. I am back too; full circle, full cycle, U'mista.

I chat with the Native woman who works at the desk. I show her my old photographs. I hear again that the other thunderbird is lying in the campground on the other side of the island. She says that totems should never be repaired or restored; they like everything else return to the earth. There it is recycled. New trees grow, new poles rise, and the process repeats. Regarding my picture of Sisook, the two-headed snake grave totem, she said that the grave had been recently rediscovered or uncovered. She confirmed it with a man working in the gift shop. She said that I could not view the totem from the road. It was hidden behind. I may be able to view it from the St. George Hospital parking lot. I didn't find it. Visitors cannot walk in the cemetery.

I sit among the potlatch masks. I feel like I have a connection to these items that have no relation to my culture. Except for perhaps those who stole and removed these items from Alert Bay. Even so, I feel at home with the masks. I know almost nothing about the potlatch or about Alert Bay, but I celebrate their return.

I write down a quote from one of the display. They are not Sammy's words, but they speak to me. It says, "I am the storage box of your thoughts, for I remember all the old tales and in my younger days. I saw things you young people never heard of."

I cannot even imagine.

I return outside to a light, misty rain. I look at the lonely wingless thunderbird faithfully guarding the entrance to the school. He does not seem powerless now. He seems honorable, majestic even, beautiful. I know that he is nearing the end of his cycle.

I decide to seek out the missing thunderbird in his final resting place. I work my way back behind the old school. I walk uphill to the new Big House and one of the world's tallest totem poles. The new Big House was reconstructed in 1999, after the old one burned down. I descend down a gravel road. I step over a barricade and continue down into the campground. I feel a presence on my right. It is almost as though Sammy was accompanying me to search for the missing thunderbird. I smile.

The campground is deserted. I cross the island and am now standing on the opposing beach. I see a boarded up building, perhaps the campground's office. I see a campsite with a hammock hanging in it.

I see a flash of color in the weeds: yellow, green, and red. It seems that the great bird had been dropped off in the most convenient of places. This appears to be a turn-around and picnic area.

I approach the grave site of this majestic bird. I remove a pink bucket and some other debris. No evidence of a head remains. I can make out where the yellow talons once were and the green feather patterns on his chest. The grizzly bear's eye stares blankly at me. The body is split open and I gaze inside the hollow body. Lichen grows in the wood. I remove a loose piece of wood. Small beetles scurry back inside to escape the light. Weeds grow up

around him. Anybody walking by would have passed by, dismissing this as a rotting painted log. I find it noble, honorable, and beautiful.

I note some flowers growing nearby in the grass. I examine the small blue flowers with light yellow centers. I laugh when I realize that these are forget-me-nots. Photographs will cause this bird to live on in the minds of the people. Sammy's pictures will remind my family of the few things we know about her. This bird would soon complete a cycle, returning to his natural state in the soil. I came to witness the end of this cycle. I will not soon forget him. I am not disappointed.

CHAPTER SEVEN: ALASKA

SAMMY CAME TO JUNEAU in the fall of 1928 to teach third and fourth grade in the Juneau public elementary school. She arrived on the steamship *Princess Charlotte* in September of 1928 after teaching for two years at Whitehall, Montana. The elementary school in Juneau was located between Fifth and Sixth streets between Seward and Franklin streets until it burned down in 1973. An average of 450 students enrolled at this school each year from 1928 to 1930. Teachers received a starting salary of about $1,260 for a nine-month contract in 1930. Sammy was chosen for this job over three hundred other applicants, according to her brother Arnold.

For at least part of her time in Juneau, she made the Gastineau Hotel on Franklin Street her home. Teachers often lived here, sharing a common bath and simple accommodations. In the early Thirties, a room here including breakfast cost about $35 a month. The hotel  allowed simple cooking on a hotplate for other meals. Near the back of the building, miners could be seen late at night as they left the A-J mine, their carbide headlamps appearing like fireflies descending from the hills. The Gastineau Hotel is now an apartment house.

Mabel Monson Burford, the Minnesota teacher who replaced Sammy in the school system, stated that teachers often left school promptly at 5 p.m. to walk up Old Basin Road to prepare coffee and hot dogs for dinner. Being avid hikers, on weekends they trekked up the Perseverance Trail or down Thane Road to the waterfalls. Old family photographs show that Sammy definitely enjoyed the hike up to the Ebner Falls on the Perseverance Trail and up Old Basin Road. Though the Alaska Gastineau Mining Company had ceased operations at the Perseverance Mine in 1921, seven years before Sammy arrived, the A-J mine bustled with activity in the Gold Creek area when she was there.

Sammy's cousin Ida Nelson stated, "Hedvig was strong for outdoor sports. She like to skate, ride horseback, hike, and picnic. She liked other sports too and dancing, but she cared most for the outdoors.

Her favorite pastime was skating."[12]
The lake front of the Mendenhall Glacier offered a great opportunity to skate in Juneau. In the Thirties, skaters could glide directly up to the glacier's vertical face and touch the glacier. Today, the glacier appears flatter, having retreated away from the lake, although it remains a popular skating destination.

---

[12] *Samuelsen Woman was Born Here*, in *Wisconsin News*, October 22, 1931: Milwaukee, WI 1.

Sammy Works at Denali Park in Interior, Alaska

Summertime for teachers in Alaska often meant adventure and travel. During the summer of 1929, Sammy and music teacher Dorothy Chisholm traveled into the interior of Alaska together, reaching McKinley (Denali) Park. After a visit there, Sammy left to visit Fairbanks until the end of June, and Dorothy went to Wrangell.

Sammy, however, returned to Denali to work for the McKinley Tourist and Transportation Company, the concessionaires of the park, for six to eight weeks before returning to Juneau. She might have gotten the job through Superintendent Harry J. Liek. They had both worked at Yellowstone the previous summer, and now Liek had replaced Harry Karstens as superintendent at Denali. Sunny found a number of

unidentified photos in Sammy's family album and was able to glean valuable information from them with the help of Jane Bryant, photo archivist at Denali. They reveal that the area that Sammy worked was certainly at Savage River Camp. At this camp, a native fur parka was available for tourists to borrow and enjoy, Bryant said. Apparently this is the parka Sammy is wearing in the photo she had taken for her Christmas card that year. Interestingly, Bryant sent Sunny two other pictures of women wearing this or a similar parka.

Another family photo showed a horse in front of a cabin. In this picture there are three tent cabins with a fourth incomplete. Jane Bryant identified this as a photo from Igloo Creek Camp and provided Sunny

with a picture of the same scene, but with the fourth cabin complete. It must have been a picture taken later than 1929, when Sammy was there.

Another picture, also from the family album, shows Sammy and the same horse in front of the first cabin. Sammy's employment might have taken her to Igloo Creek Camp as well as to Savage River Camp. It's also possible these were taken earlier in the summer when she visited the area before she was employed.

Another family photo is of a scene that was next to the other pictures of Igloo Creek and Savage River. Bryant thought that this was perhaps a scene along the Teklanika River. If you

were to ride horseback from Savage River to Igloo Creek, you would go by the Teklanika.

Bryant also studied another family photo of a road. She said, "The road is inconclusive but the trees are very much like McKinley Park. It could well be the park road looking east and going downhill into the

Savage River drainage. It all looks very familiar. My guess it is McKinley Park, near mile 13 or 14."

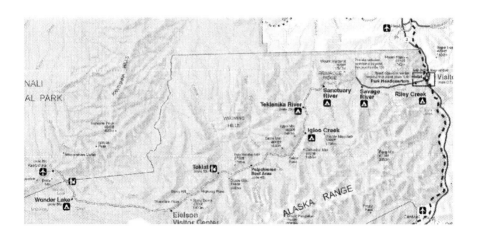

This map shows where the Savage River camp is located. It is 12 miles from the McKinley Station and served as a main tourist area, since the hotel that was planned had not yet been built. Savage River is currently as far as you can drive your own car into the park. Igloo Creek is about mile 35 on the road. The road had been finished through mile 38 the summer Sammy was there. Work on the park road was also going on.

Note also the location of the Teklanika River, also a camp area. She surely also had been at the Sanctuary River Camp.

AUTHORIZED RATES for

Authorized rates for pack train and camp accommodations in Mount McKinley National Park, Alaska, season 1924.

Quoted rates for trips and accommodations are for minimum parties of 6 or more persons.

Trip No. 1—McKinley Park Station to Savage River Camp—34 miles made by saddle animal train. Authorized round trip fare................$16.00

Trip No. 2—Savage River Camp to Igloo Creek Camp—18 miles made by saddle animal train. Authorized round trip fare................$26.00

Trip No. 3—Igloo Creek Camp to Toklat River Camp—30 miles made by saddle animal train. Authorized round trip fare................$38.00

Twenty pounds of baggage carried free per person on above trips.

Authorized rates for meals and lodging are as follows:

SAVAGE RIVER CAMP
Lodging
    Two persons in tent house, each................$1.25
    One person in tent house................1.75
Meals
    Breakfast................$1.85
    Lunch................2.00
    Dinner................2.00

IGLOO CREEK CAMP
Lodging
    In large sleeping tent, per person................$1.25
    One person in tent house................2.00
Meals
    Breakfast................$2.00
    Lunch................2.00
    Dinner................2.00

TOKLAT RIVER CAMP
Lodging
    In large sleeping tent, per person................$1.25
    One person in tent house................2.00
Meals
    Breakfast................$2.00
    Lunch................2.00
    Dinner................2.00

For special short trips or for parties of less than 6 persons: Guides, packers, and cooks with horse including board and feed, per day................$20.00
    Pack horses including feed, each, per day................8.00
    Saddle horses, including feed, each per day................10.00

Lodgings and meals for party members, extra.

Main entrance to McKinley National Park is at Mile 248, Alaska Railroad.

Beyond Savage River Camp, parties for the Mt. McKinley trip should register as far in advance as possible. Assignments will be made in order of registration.

This photo is the rate schedule for the park from 1924.[13] Sammy was here in 1929, but even in 1924 visitors could travel from Savage River to Igloo Creek on horseback. Sammy definitely went on one of these

---

[13] National Park Service, *Circular of General Information Regarding: Mount McKinley National Park, Alaska: Season from June 1 to September 15, 1929*: U.S. Government Printing Office.

trips in 1929 when she worked and perhaps led tourists on some of these trips that summer.

There are a number of photos in the family album that show methods of transportation in the park that summer. In one of the  photos, there is a bus that looks like an antique limousine. Each compartment has its own door. It has been identified as a Fageol Safety Coach, brought to Alaska by the Mt. McKinley Tourist and Transportation Company (MMT&TCo). Before the company upgraded to Studebaker buses in the 1930s, this was used to transport visitors into the park. The picture shows one of the two such buses

 that were used. Another photo shows a whole row of tourist cars; part of the concession company's touring car fleet.

Two stagecoaches were also used to transport tourists. Denali acquired two stagecoaches from Yellowstone for this purpose. Bryant studied this picture from the family album and concluded that this is from Savage River. The man driving the stagecoach is Lou Corbley, an MT&TCo. employee and later Chief Ranger at Mt. McKinley National

Park. She said there were four stagecoaches in all. Bryant sent Sunny a

 picture which showed the stagecoach again with the same horses as well as the bus seen in the family picture.

Other photos reveal what life was like for Sammy while working at

Denali. Sunny had difficulty finding Sammy in some of the pictures until she noticed that Sammy frequently appeared in a plaid jacket, a white shirt and a black necktie. From this observation she was able to look for the distinctive jacket and find her. This is a picture of Sammy in Juneau sporting

the identifiable jacket, shirt and tie.

This picture is apparently Sammy wearing her jacket sitting with mosquito netting around her head. Mosquitoes infested the area that summer and everyone wore mosquito netting for protection.

Horses were also used for transport. These photos are probably from a riding trip near the Savage River with either a touring group or co-workers. Sammy is wearing her plaid jacket again.

This family picture shows Sammy on a dog sled. This picture was a big mystery to Jane Bryant. She felt the sled was odd. "It is either an old wreck or a new, unfinished sled. My guess is that it is an older sled in need of repair and is sitting on top of at least one log dog house (left side). The trees in the background are quite large for McKinley Park, but could be from near the headquarters area, where the National Park Service sled dog kennel was located." The kennels at Denali were being constructed that summer (1929) at their current site, but sled dog demonstrations were not held until 1938. They are performed daily today.

In a letter Sammy reflected about her time in the park. "Spent one summer way up in the interior," she wrote. "There were plenty of mountain sheep, fox, caribou, grizzly bears, etc. to make it interesting."[14] She returned to Juneau in the fall bringing with her gold

---

[14] *Memories of Alaska*, in *Minot Daily News*. Oct 21, 1931: Minot, ND.

dust she had panned from a placer mine giving "proof of her experience" from her summer travels.

At the end of the summer, Sammy left the interior traveling on the Richardson Highway. She went to Valdez, then took the boat back to Juneau to start her second year of teaching. In a few months she would meet Anne LeRoi, who would become her best friend.

Anne, a nurse from Portland, Oregon, had traveled to Wrangell in October 1929 and had become the superintendent at the Wrangell General Hospital. One source said Anne met Sammy at the Wrangell hospital, but the meeting most likely took place later, after February 1930, when Anne moved to Juneau to work at St. Ann's Hospital. Upon moving, she registered at the Alaskan Hotel, just a block from the Gastineau Hotel where Sammy lived.

Though it's not known exactly how or when they met, the meeting most likely took place on Feb. 15, 1930, during a Juneau blizzard. Sammy wrote in her diary a year later, "Just think, it's been just a year since I met Anne. It seems that I knew her always". A family photograph shows the pair in winter facing the Juneau Elementary School on Franklin Street. The picture clearly shows historical buildings in the

background, such as the Sweeney Apartments and St. Nicolas Russian Orthodox Church.

The two women became close friends even though they did not know each other for any great length of time. Sammy left Juneau on June 13 to attend the Chicago Normal School for the summer, not returning until August 26, ready to begin her third year of teaching in the Juneau Elementary School. After being back in Juneau for a month, she discovered that she had contracted tuberculosis. Anne quit her job at St. Ann's hospital to accompany her south to a drier climate. Anne thought she could find work and care for Sammy as well. They left Juneau together on the steamship *Admiral Rogers* on Oct. 2, 1930. The women originally sailed for Laguna Beach, California, but then headed for the hot dry climate of Phoenix, Arizona, where they were both murdered in 1931 by Winnie Ruth Judd.

In Alaska, the two women were well known and well liked. According to the *Juneau Empire*, "News of the tragedy appalled both child and adult as regarded Miss Samuelson who was so favorably and widely known." The Juneau paper also stated that Anne, a popular nurse, had a host of friends in Juneau. The *Alaska Weekly* stated that everybody who knew Sammy and Anne "loved them and regarded them highly." Newspapers from around the country carried quotes from many people who said they knew them. It's possible that, because of the notoriety of the crime, people who barely knew them said they recalled them. But it's also possible that, in a small city like Juneau, that they really were known to many prominent Alaskans.

An article in the *Anchorage Daily Times* stated that former Juneau residents Mr. and Mrs. Bob Ellis knew Sammy. Bob Ellis, an aviator, made the first Seattle-to-Juneau non-stop flight on April 15, 1929, and later founded Ellis Airlines in Ketchikan. Soon after his historic flight, he started taking passengers up in his seaplane for twenty-minute tours of the glacial ice cap, charging them ten dollars a head. Sammy may have taken this tour, either as a paying passenger or as a friend of the pilot. When she was sick in Phoenix, she wrote to some friends in Landa, North Dakota: "In Juneau, we did a lot of plane riding, friends of mine being connected with the airways. It is the best way to see the country, flying over immense glaciers, lakes, and mountains, gives one the most wonderful thrills."[15] At least one of these tours took place in the spring of 1930, according to *Alaskan Aviation History* by Robert W. Stevens: "Bob Ellis has a busy day with the Taku on Sunday, May 11, 1930 in Juneau. Going to the Pacific American Fisheries Plant on Excursion Inlet in the morning, the pilot carried forty passengers aloft on sightseeing trips. For a round trip out of Juneau he had carried Miss Anne LeRoy, Miss Hedvig Samuelson, Margaret "Peg" Ellis, Larry Parks and AB Cot Hayes. About 2 he returned to the capital city to bring in his round-trippers and gas up."[16] AB Cot Hayes was the manager for the airlines in Juneau. Alaskan political figures such as John Troy, who later served as governor of Alaska, apparently knew Sammy and helped raise money for her departure from Juneau. Troy at the time was publisher of the *Daily Alaska Empire*. After her death, he described Sammy as a "little beam of sunshine" and said her friends had rallied around her. "When she suddenly needed to leave Juneau

---

[15] *Memories of Alaska*, in *Minot Daily News*, Oct 21, 1931: Minot, ND, 10

after contracting tuberculosis, she was without funds since she had just returned from her summer in Chicago. Anne LeRoi volunteered to take Sammy to Arizona since she thought she could obtain work there and we paid the expenses of both of them," Troy said.[17] This account, which seems to indicate the money was raised solely by Troy and other friends, is in conflict with other versions of the story, which assert the funds were actually raised by the board of education and the school teachers of Juneau or by general donations from Juneau townspeople.

One of Sammy's supportive friends in Alaska was Captain Austin Lathrop, a wealthy theater owner, moviemaker, miner, newspaper

publisher, and political figure. It is unknown how they met. He owned the *Fairbanks New Miner* and a large Alaska movie theater chain. He also financed the first film filmed in Alaska, *The Chechakos*, in 1923. He managed a mine near Healy, near Denali. Lathrop apparently gave Sammy money when she contracted TB and left

Juneau, according to a newspaper timeline of the events leading up to Sammy's death. One timeline entry reads: "Austin Lathrop raises $1000—some say $2500—for Sammy. They pay the expenses of both Anne LeRoi and Sammy to head south."[18]

---

[16] Stevens, Robert W., *Alaskan Aviation History*. 1990, Des Moines, Wash: Polynyas Press. V.

[17] "Sunshine" to Juneau, in *Minot Daily News*. Oct 22, 1931: Minot, ND. 2

[18] *Trunk Murder Jealousy is Revealed*, in *Chicago American*. Oct 23, 1931: Chicago. 34.

In September 1930, Captain Lathrop wired Sammy from Healy, Alaska: "Received your letter today. Deeply grieved over your condition. Hope with rest and good care that you will soon restore your good health and be able to resume your work. Am mailing you check for five hundred stop. Will be glad to hear from you, Signed, A.E. Lathrop.[19]

Cap is one of the most famous men in Alaska. In the territory's early days, he played an active role in resisting statehood, and his character appears in the book and movie, *Ice Palaces*. Despite his celebrity, few details about him are known and there are no archives holding his papers.

Anthony J. Dimond, who was a representative of the Alaska Territory in 1929, introduced a bill that year to establish a teacher's retirement fund and apparently knew Sammy. His papers, archived in Fairbanks, reveal that he wrote to her while she was living in Phoenix on Feb. 1, 1931, saying, "I know that you are going to be ok and I still marvel at your good luck in having such a splendid pal."[20] He wrote again on March 26, saying, "I was particularly touched by the phrase in your letter to Gertrude in which you wondered if the members of the legislature would miss you. We

---

[19] *Letters of Friendship to Miss Samuelson Bared*, in *Los Angeles Evening Herald*, Oct 22, 1931: Los Angeles 11.

[20] *Letters of Friendship to Miss Samuelson Bared*, in *Los Angeles Evening Herald*, Oct 22, 1931: Los Angeles, 11

miss you so greatly that is if we had the magic of securing one wish and only one, it would be cheerfully extended in wishing you sound and well and in the city of Juneau. Good night. Sleep Well."[21]

After Sammy's death, newspapers looking to exploit every sensational angle said she knew famous actor John Barrymore and his wife, the actress Dolores Costello, and had been invited to take a cruise with them on their yacht *Infanta*. This was a stretch, but there was some basis for the story. The Barrymores vacationed in Alaska waters in June 1931, "seeking rest" while Sammy lay ill in Arizona. "Society woman" June Cann, living in Seattle, wrote a letter to Sammy in September 1931 stating, "John and Dolores Barrymore visited us for 27 days on their yacht *Infanta* and it was sure fun to have them, and if we go south this winter they want us to visit them in Beverly Hills. Could you go along with us on our yacht?"[22] June Cann was the one who apparently knew the Barrymores.

It's not clear how Sammy knew June Cann, but the historical record holds clues as to the connection. Sammy's diary contained a list of addresses in the back including: Mrs. J. Cann, The Northcliff Apartments, 308 West, corner Seneca and Boren, Seattle, WA. Also, the 1930 US census lists James Cann, married with no occupation, at the Gastineau Hotel, the same place that Sammy lived. James Cann actually owned part of the hotel, but his family lived elsewhere. Assuming James Cann was related to June Cann, he might well have met Sammy at the hotel and introduced her to June. James Cann sold

---

[21] Ibid.

his share of the hotel to John Biggs in May of 1930. He hoped to reunite with his family and resume mining activities at the Apex-El Nido mines in Alaska.

Sammy had a knack for making friends with people from all walks of life. Another prominent person she befriended was Thomas T.K. Frelinghuysen, a noted sculptor from New Jersey. She met him on a steamer, and he wrote to her for months, discussing sending her books and money. However, when contacted by the press after Sammy's death, he denied any personal involvement with her.

Sunny's First Visit to Juneau in September 1999

I watch the back of Marc's head as he walks out the door. I crack open one of the fortune cookies remaining on the table, "Explore the back roads of the north with a new friend," it reads.

"Men Fight over What? But, I hide myself to the wastelands of the north to try to forget-Rickey" – Oct. 15, 1931, the last entry in Hedvig Samuelson's Diary.[23]

Damn, I really hate men right now. I just want to forget about them. It is time to leave these things behind. I compromised so many times during the past couple of months. Lofty ideas; I take the dog to bed instead.

I roll over in bed and eye the alarm clock; 4:00. Emptiness fills me. I feel hollow. I decide to get up and call the airline on a whim. I find that I can use my frequent flier miles that I got from the divorce and fly to

---

[22] *Victim Invited to Visit Stars*, in *Los Angeles Evening Express*. Oct. 22, 1931: Los Angeles, 3.

[23] *Trunk Slayer Has Killed Self, Police Believe*, in *Chicago Daily Tribune*, Oct. 22, 1931: Chicago, IL.

Juneau the following day. Ah, salvation and vengeance all at once, I figure. An urgent need to get out overcomes me again. I feel the pull to head to Juneau. I want to see if anything can be found there. Maybe, I just need to escape. I consider the possibility that this is running away, but I dismiss it. I don't care.

Time is of the essence, I reason as I hurry into work. I carry all of the photos that I collected of everything that could possibly be Alaska. My colleagues give me that look out of the corner of their eyes as if to say, "Have you felt your forehead today for fever?" They say instead, "you make the best scrapbooks" or "how interesting." Noon rolls around and I paste all of the copies of the pictures into my book. I determine that it would be my only guide in Alaska, nothing else. What else could I need anyway? On the first page of my scrapbook, I place a picture of Sammy standing in the middle of a field in front of some mountains. She is wearing Native skins. Underneath the picture she wrote, "Merry Christmas from Hedvig Samuelson" in a very fancy script. It appears that she wrote it on a ruler and added the g afterwards.

I pack very little. Luggage only weighs you down, I decide. A raincoat, pants, fleece, long underwear, good boots and socks are put in my pack. It is enough.

I spend most of the evening putting other odds and ends into my book. A map of Juneau, copies of articles that I collected, and addresses of old teachers in Juneau are included. I mull over the scrapbook that I have constructed. I run out to buy black and white film at midnight. Color seems inappropriate for Juneau. I will see this place in color, but it must be recorded and remembered in black and white. It was the way Sammy saw and remembered it.

I review a letter to Mr. and Mrs. Bogstie of Landa, North Dakota, which was reprinted in the *Minot Daily News*, Oct. 21, 1931, entitled *Memories of Alaska*, as I try to go to sleep:

"Since I saw you that summer so long ago (about four years) I've spent most of my time in Alaska," Miss Samuelson wrote. "Had some wonderful experiences there, which at least leave me with a lot of memories. You would love the scenery, gorgeous mountains and blue water with little islands everywhere. Spent one summer way up in the interior…There were plenty of mountain sheep, fox, caribou, grizzly bears, etc. to make it interesting.

In Juneau we did a lot of plane riding. Friends of mine being connected with the airways. It is the best way to see the country, flying over immense glaciers, lakes and mountains, gives one the most wonderful thrills. Then we took some wonderful trips by water in and among the islands."[24]

I enter the plane. The plane appears to be jammed packed. I find my seat in-between an elderly fellow and woman. There is nothing quite like being stuck in-between two people on a long flight. I sigh and think this is going to be the longest six hours. I plan to ignore both of these individuals. I successfully keep my nose in "Cakes and Ale" (a book rumored to be in Sammy's apartment at the time of her death) until the meals roll by.

I examine the woman sitting next to me in the window seat. She is definitely not as old as I had originally thought, maybe 50. Her hair is a radiant red, pulled up into a girlish pigtail. She is trim and is dressed in

---

[24] *Memories of Alaska*, in *Minot Daily News*. October 21, 1931:Minot, ND

jeans and a navy sweatshirt. She pulls out this technical looking reading material. There are round colored circles that I don't know quite what to make of. Finally she speaks to me and says that they are fossil samples. I say that I am going to Juneau.

She says, "I hope you brought a shotgun with you. Those bears will rip your arms off. I had a friend who refused to carry a gun and was working on Admiralty Island and was attacked by a bear. She lost both her arms." I look at her with some disbelief. She continues, "I have worked just about everywhere in Alaska for various oil companies. I tell them the best locations to dig after I collect fossil samples. I am going to Barrow on the Arctic Ocean.'

"How do you get there?" I ask.

"Oh, the oil company has their own planes. They fly workers in and out each week to Anchorage. They work for a month up there and then have two weeks of vacation. The oil company is the only one allowed up there," she replies. 'I work up here when and if I feel like it. I am retired in Florida now." This woman I later discovered was Anita Harris, a world famous geologist.

I arrive and stay at a hostel on 614 Harris Street and pay $7/night. The first night I read from writings by Mabel Monson Burford, *Juneau Stories of Teaching on the Last Frontier*.[25] Mabel was the teacher who replaced Sammy when she became ill and had to leave Alaska.

I am ready for my first day in Juneau.

---

[25] Burford, Mabel, *Mabel Monson Burford, in Juneau Stories of Teaching on the Last Frontier*, 1993, Juneau Retired Teachers' Association: Juneau, AK p. 7-11

9/8/99 Old Basin Road, Perseverance Falls, Ebner Falls (Sunny's writing expanded by her from a diary entry)

Rain. I step outside the Hostel to find rain. Low clouds cover the mountain thinly, unevenly. I couldn't believe it when I walked by the St. Nicolas Church and the house. I wasn't looking for it and it was 1 block from the hostel. It really is a steep slope which doesn't seem to be the case in the picture I have with me. I found that the Gastineau Hotel was still here. It is now the Gastineau Apartments and has some shops below. Supposedly, it's retirement or senior housing now. One picture definitely shows the playground and elementary school. The house on the right is the same house

that Hedvig and Anne LeRoi are standing next to in the picture. The old postcard picture shows St. Anne's Hospital at the far right corner. The school is no longer there since it burned in 1972.

I consult my book and see again a quote by Mabel Monson:

"In the thirties, the young adults about town were avid hikers . . . . Teachers after 5 would leave directly from school and hike up Basin Road to prepare coffee and hot dogs for their suppers. On weekends, they would hike up Perseverance or down Thane Road to the waterfalls." – Mabel Monson Burford

I start up the hill above the hostel and turn left and hike up to the dead end on Harris Street. I turn right on Gold Street and head up the hill to Basin Road. There is a dead end up the end of Gold Street. It looks like it might have once been a park. The road turns sharply right and becomes Basin Road. Colorful modest houses line the road. Everybody seems to have a kayak or two tucked under their deck.

There is this cute wooden one-lane bridge. It runs next to a gully  which is below on the left. There is a three-tiered wooden rail fixed to a timber along the left to the west. Granite Creek runs below. The water is crystal clear and blue. I examine my book. Sammy sits on a similar looking bridge. It is the same, but there is no safety rail. She straddles the timber with her hands between her knees. She wears a white hat and a plaid coat. I imagine that it is several shades of brown. The creek is more visible below in the picture. There are fewer trees than in the Twenties. I know it is the same place. I am on the right road. A tour bus passes me on the bridge. I assume it is going to the mine museum.

I walk along the road wondering where somebody might cook hot dogs and coffee. I listen for voices from the Twenties. Women laughing. I do not hear them.

I turn down a gully near a log chute of some sort. The water is blue, but dirty. The railroad tracks have been replaced and made into a walking trail. I turn onto them and backtrack for a while. The rain falls. A black Labrador bounds up behind me. I pet him enthusiastically and ask him whether he plans to join me for the walk. His master comes along soon afterward, jogging along the slippery planks of the old railroad bed.

I turn back and decide to continue down Old Basin Road. On the right there appears to be some sort of water supply area for Juneau. Signs appear from time to time to warn about littering and pollution. I walk on glancing at the creek, noting the rocks.

I remember seeing a picture of Anne LeRoi and Sammy on a rock by a river. It is definitely Alaska, but it's not definitely here. Anne looks chunky and is wearing shorts. I don't have a copy of the picture. I have only seen it in newspapers. The only thing I remember of Sammy is that she is wearing an ugly plaid skirt, but the thing I remember most is the socks! It looks like she has rolled her socks down into a tight circular band at the ankles. They are both wearing the ugliest black shoes. I examine my own shoes, Gore-Tex boots that my Dad gave me for my birthday. My feet are dry, I smile. I examine the rocks on Granite Creek. Maybe they did picnic somewhere down here once. I look again for a place to build a fire.

I come to the Perseverance Mine at the end Perseverance Trail. I head up the first switchback and come to the opening of an old mine. It's wood and I walk on in. There is a wire barrier inside. The Perseverance Mine operated from 1885-1895 and was rebuilt in 1900. It burned down in 1912. The mine was in operation until 1921. So, the mine was not in operation more than likely when teachers came to walk here. I walk up and continue along the trail. I come to a sign at the beginning of the trail, it says something like Warning, Avalanche area. Things are very beautiful and historic here, but also it is very dangerous.

It continues to rain, now harder. I tread uphill and start to feel quite warm. I foolishly remove my leather hat and my hair gets soaked. The front legs of my jeans become wet. More warning signs. There is a rock face to my left. Is this shale? It is black, and sometimes there is quartz intermingled among the rocks. There is a waterfall. I think about taking a picture of it. I decide not to since most waterfall pictures end up less impressive than they look. I put my hat over my wet hair. I notice shiny wet bunchberry along the trail.

The rock face to my right is sharp and steep. I think that it might have been cut out manually to make this trail. I don't know. In other places, the water runs down the rocks in miniature waterfalls. In all cases water drips off of every rock. I am soaked.

I see a sign that says Ebner Falls. It is the waterfall that I saw from the trail a ways back. The rain slows and my wet loose jeans begin to dry as my legs move around freely inside them once again. My hair begins to dry and I let it down loose. I turn right and work my way down a small slope. Across some tiny streams, I end up in a small picnic area. I put my camera on one of the damp picnic tables and try out the automatic timer. I stand next to a tree with moss on it. The falls swerve around the picnic area and then fall steeply down. I stand at the top and look down. The trees are tight here and Death feels very close. I think about falling off the falls to my death. I contemplate jumping. I step back abruptly. To my right is a small, calm pool, with a tiny 2- foot waterfall. It is quite the contrast from the thundering falls that stand to the front of me.

I turn back and walk up stream. The clear water appears blue often. There is a large boulder in the creek. I think again about the picture of Anne LeRoi and Sammy sitting on the rock somewhere near Juneau. But Granite Creek is too narrow here. I put the camera on the rock and set the timer. I walk upstream and model myself on a rock.

I head back to the Perseverance Trail. I continue down the trail. The trail widens and I cross several bridges that cross the creek. One has a label saying it was made in Minnesota. I hear the call of the library and the microfilm that I came here to scour. I turn back and pick up my pace. Quite the uneventful hike really.

The gully is now on my left. I hurry back down past the Ebner Falls turnoff. I start singing. (What the hell was I singing? Will everybody here kindly step to the rear and let a winner lead the way?) I pretend that Sammy is walking down the trail with me. I imagine holding her hand. I wonder what she would talk about. I ask her questions out loud. A person wearing Mukluks and a yellow slicker passes me heading in the other direction. I abruptly shut up. I laugh out loud.

I stop abruptly. My heart skips a beat. I see an old rotting timber on the trail, apparently an old barrier of some sort. There is no other indication that any other timbers were ever here. It is covered with green moss, split in several places. The timber is sinking into the moist ground. Behind it grows some scruffy, tree-like brush. It grows perilously on the edge of the cliff. It grips the rock for life and has grown short and thick. I barely see the Ebner Falls through the brush. It starts to rain again.

I pull out my book and stand close to the rock face on the right. Drops of rain fall onto the book. I see another picture of Sammy sitting on a timber. The timber is raised by small blocks of wood. There is a waterfall in the gully below. I study the rocks in the picture. I walk down the path to get a better look at the Ebner Falls. The waterfall zig-  zags down the black channel. Mustard colored moss covers some of the rocks. In the middle is a large boulder. I examine the picture from the Twenties. I see the same boulder! Waterfalls are commonplace in Alaska. It is amazing to identify the same waterfall!

I rush back to the timber. Certainly that brush could have grown up during the last seventy years. The timbers must have served as a barrier for hikers in the past. This piece of timber was the only remnant. The rest of the ridge railing fell to the depths of the cliff below. It is amazing to think that Sammy may have actually sat on this very timber. It is raining and the timber is saturated. I sit on it anyway. I smile.

I start back along the trail staring back at the timber several times. I imagine Sammy sitting on the timber. I feel a presence as I continue along the path. I feel her walking next to me. I hear her breathing. I hear a faint voice. I hear laughter. I laugh.

09/10/1999 Mount Roberts

On Friday, I set out about 11:30 up the Mount Roberts Trail from town. At first I thought that this would be more appropriately called Mount Mud since it was extremely muddy and 3.5 miles straight up to the tram. The weather was partly clear but soon clouded up above the tram. I thought I'd take the tram down. I wasn't extremely impressed. I ran into two fellows from the hostel who invited me to go with them to the peak. It was supposed to be an additional 2 miles. Change!? The sun was out and there were rocky paths and meadows. Pretty yellow leaves, clear streams. Snow patches, marmots, ptarmigans. People were up looking for bear on the hillside. Fog was hanging along the side of the mountain. It was an adverse climb. One of the guys was from Scotland and had a huge pack. He planned to camp near the summit. We came to an area that looked like the moon. No plant life, just black shale. The landscape changed several times; bushy to flat and barren and with white quartz. The path was marked by green flags. You really needed these. It started to rain and the fog drifted in. You couldn't see 15 feet in front of you. Ptarmigans were along the rocks. I had never seen these before but knew very well what these were. There were a pair of them walking along the ridge. The male had a red spot under his eye. I just loved them for some reason. Conditions became more adverse as we neared the first summit – Gastineau Peak. I went ahead since I was afraid of becoming too wet and chilled. I reached the summit and picked up some white quartz that had just split in half. I took both pieces. We continued on for it was 1 more mile to the real summit, but we kept losing the trail. Finally, we gave up and headed back.

9/11/1999 Mendenhall Glacier West – Skater's Cabin

I hiked the western side of the Mendenhall Glacier on Saturday. I stopped to examine the Skater's Cabin, a popular place to ice skate in

the winter.

I loved being here. Apparently, it burned in 1988 and was rebuilt right away. The stone foundation said 1936, but I am willing to bet there was a structure of some sort here before that. I was sure Sammy had skated from this place in this picture. It is no doubt the Mendenhall Glacier from the west.

Skater's Cabin

Voices
Echoing through these walls
Retelling tales of years past

Laughter
Heard around the fire
Yesterday, Today, and Tomorrow

I continued on to the West Glacier Trail from here. I was instructed by the guy at the information booth to make noise since the salmon run was slowing and the bears were looking for "something new to do." I made up the verse about the skater's cabin as I hiked. I made another verse as well, just in case the bears were listening. This one I called *Love Lupine:*

Lupine on the side of the road
Standing alone, erect
Waiting for possible sun.
Finding none, it continues to wait.
Lupine on the side of the road.

I have always liked lupines. I have never seen them growing as scattered and single as on the Glacier Spur Road.

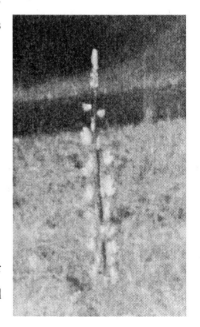

The hike on the West Glacier Trail was level and easy for a long time. The rain was light, but constant. The trail grew steeper and overlooked the glacier from above. I made an error and walked right off the path and followed flags, much like on Mount Roberts. I assumed because it was marked that it was the path, but it was not. I came to an 8-foot rock face without any footholds at all. It was quite a trick to get up on that rock. I must have tried for at least 30 minutes. I did it, but the trail grew more adverse. Finally, I slid off a rock into a pine tree, and decided to turn back. I had no choice but to slide down that wet rock face. When I got back to the path, I realized that I missed an easy switchback. I just walked off of the path!

I walked another hour. The path was better, but was confusing when it crossed streams and waterfalls. More guesswork. Great views directly over the glacier though. Finally the path went straight up wet rock with water running down it. I knew I could make it up, but would probably have to slide down it. I was feeling slightly sick and was tired so I made the decision to turn back. Even so, the walk lasted 5 hours. I wasn't cold until I got on the bus. Then I froze and was frozen for hours after that.

9/12/99 Morning, Thane Road

Stiff and tired I walked up Thane Road this morning after breakfast. I thought an easy walk might loosen me up a bit. Not at all! I grew stiffer and more tired each step of the way. I'd say I walked about 2.5-3 miles down and back. There were some nice waterfalls down there. Forget-Me-Not's, and some other flowers grew along the road. This road goes along the channel. It's an avalanche danger zone. Big signs saying "Do Not Stop."

I saw an eagle on a post at the beach. Gee, the beach was dirty and polluted. I walked on the beach. Tons of barnacles, shells and seaweed. Blade shell-like gook everywhere.

I walked down to the mouth of a small but vigorous stream. It was at the bottom of a large waterfall. This part of it was shallow and fast. Salmon were frantically trying to swim up this stream. They would shelter themselves behind rocks to rest and then push forward. Most of the time, they would flip over and get washed back towards the channel. A lot of them seemed to be swimming in place. Primal instincts. Funny thing (or perhaps sad) was that there was no pool for the salmon here. Well, maybe a 4-foot by 4-foot one. Only a few small ones were in there.

9/12/99 Afternoon, Sick in Juneau

I felt awful about 2:30. I checked back into the Inn at the Waterfront and took a hot bath. I got upgraded to a very nice room since somebody else was very sick in the other one. I got under the white down comforter and thought it was the best place I'd ever been.

Sixty-nine years ago in 1930, probably the second or third week of September, Sammy got sick here too and was forced to leave. I am not that sick, but it is interesting to be sick here as well and experience this. Who wouldn't get sick here in the rain? One is wet, all of the time. I guess September here is the worst. Ironically, the sun was out for the first time this afternoon.

Marlene and Patsy Ann

The sun was out Sunday night and I made my way back to the Inn at the Waterfront. I talked to this woman who was curled up next to the Patsy Ann statue. Patsy Ann was a deaf terrier dog that met all of the boats in the Thirties and late Twenties. Mabel Monson said Patsy Ann was there when she arrived in 1930 in October. Marlene told me about her dogs and her experience in moving to

115

the interior. She had been in SE for twenty-odd years and wouldn't think of living anywhere else. She called me at the hotel and left me a few names of historians in town. I didn't have time to call them. She said I fit right in here! The picture is of me with Patsy Ann, not Marlene.

Gold Dust 9/12/99 Evening

Daily Alaska Empire, Aug. 22, 1929, p. 2, "Juneau Teacher Returns from Summer in Interior."

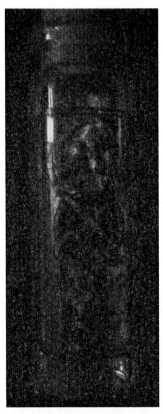

"One of her most thrilling experiences was visiting the different kinds of mines in the vicinity of Fairbanks and actually panning gold from a placer mine. As proof of her experience, Miss Samuelson returned with some samples of gold dust."[26]

I had bought a few vials of gold flakes to bring back for those who worked the desk for me while I was gone. What awful, dusky souvenirs, I had thought. However, I dropped by the Juneau Public Library and found this article. Now, these dusky souvenirs seemed appropriate. I couldn't help but smile.

Evidence of my experience!

---

[26] *Juneau Teacher Returns from Summer in Interior*, in *Daily Alaska Empire*, August 22, 1929: Juneau, AK p2

9/13/1999 Mabel Monson Burford

I went out to visit Mabel Burford at 3:00 in the afternoon. She was waiting for me outside of her garage. She lived up past Auke Bay on the Glacier Highway. I was late. I made two mistakes with the bus. I think that she worried that I wasn't coming. My first impression was that this must be the spryest 94-year-old I had ever seen.

She had a beautiful condo with a deck overlooking Spaulding Bay. Islands, boats and seagulls were easily viewed.

She built a fire in her fireplace and served me some hot apple cider.

She showed me her pictures from her early years in Juneau. She arrived in early October of 1930 to replace Sammy in the school system. Her photo album had a seal skin cover and it was in fantastic shape. Somebody gave her the skins and she had it cut to make this photo album. It was soft with very fine hair.

Her pictures included shots of her trip on the Mendenhall Glacier (which took several days to hike). She had to pass a physical exam and test to make sure she could endure the trip. Based on my own experience on the west glacier trail, I could appreciate that. That trip took a lot out of me.

She had pictures of the Old Basin Road and hiking there. The trails looked much like the picture at the beginning of my book. Mabel thought these were the Old Basin Road and the Perseverance Trail.

She had pictures of her trip in the early Thirties to the interior which were much like Sammy's. She spoke of her friend Alice (Alice Erbe?) who was always going somewhere and talking the other teachers into going on trips. I believe that she was the one who went with her on her trip into the interior early in her days in Juneau.

Mabel took a boat to Hawaii in 1934! Alone! I found this unbelievable to travel by boat from Juneau to Hawaii, let alone in 1934.

She had pictures of hiking (and tobogganing) on the Mount Roberts trail. They did most of their hiking up there in the winter. I could appreciate that as well after the tough hike up there last Friday.

This woman was in phenomenal shape in her day and I believe in this time as well. She married Jack in 1945 and quit teaching. Jack was into boats and so eventually they ended up in Auke Bay. She never had any children and she said she was the last in her line.

A Minnesota girl, too. She grew up near Watertown, Minnesota. She got her teaching certificate in Winona. She taught for 2 years near

Bemidji. She had a brother near Hibbing. She said she liked the bluffs near Winona, but Alaska was so much better, but she didn't know it at the time.

When Sammy fell ill and needed to leave for a drier climate, Mabel got the job. She got in her car and drove to Seattle to catch the steamship *Yukon* to Juneau. She arrived in Juneau in early October and it was a beautiful stretch of sunny weather. She had playground supervisor duties with another teacher and she couldn't understand why this teacher kept saying, "This is such beautiful weather." Mabel was accustomed to sunny Minnesota days. The other teacher said, "Wait until the rains come." "What?" she said, "Does it rain here?"

DOES IT RAIN HERE?!

We laughed about that quite a bit.

Mabel gave me an ivory Billiken. She claimed that I should rub its stomach and make a wish. If I didn't get my wish, then turn it over and spank it. I had seen these items around Juneau. I will need to look up its tradition. She said it was for good luck.

This is the way to be 94!

Apparently, Mabel was absolutely thrilled with my visit. She even skipped her meeting that morning because of "this very special guest." It's interesting because she wanted me to sign her guest book and I wanted her to sign my book as well. Kind of like opposite hero worship or something.

She said that she always felt so bad that because of Sammy's misfortune she was able to come to Juneau, Alaska. For if Sammy had not contracted TB in September of 1930, Mabel would never have come to Juneau, which she has called home for 70 years now.

She talked about the strange twists of fate that so often occurred in her life including the prominence of the number 13. She always considered it a lucky sort of number even though her husband died on Friday the 13th.

Anyway, she said how remarkable that I would come to visit her on the 13th of the month. She said it was very important for her to meet a relative of Sammy's for without her she would have never come to Juneau at all.

I thought the visit was important for me too in a spiritual sense. I felt like even though Mabel's experiences were unique for her life, that in a way, many of her experiences were much like Sammy's were and might have been. By talking to her, I felt I knew a bit more about Sammy and what her life might have been like.

It was strange to think that this fall, Sammy could have been 96. She really could still be living in Auke Bay as Mabel is. I am willing to bet Sammy would have visited Cuba and Hawaii in the Thirties as Mabel did. I bet she would have visited South America like she said in one of her letters had she continued to live.

Mabel said that she also kept a diary when she first came to Juneau in 1930. However, when Sammy was killed, she was upset about the publicity. Apparently, the newspapers picked out certain things in her diary and misconstrued them and made her look very bad. Fearing that might someday happen to her, she threw her diary in the Yukon River.

She never kept a diary again. But, she said to this day she regrets the loss of this log of a very important part of her life.

Fortunately, Sunny chose to keep her diaries which have made this book possible.

January 8, 2000 Addendum:

I learned today that Mabel Monson Burford passed away on Dec. 22, 1999 in her home. I consider myself extremely lucky to have met this extraordinary woman and heard some of the stories from her life. She made quite an impression on me.

9/13/99 Brotherhood Bridge

It seems I had traveled full circle now. After leaving Mabel, I returned to Auke Bay to Deharts for the bus. I had an hour. I talked with the guys working in Deharts and asked about the Brotherhood Bridge. One said it was about 3 miles down the road. I hitched a ride with this guy and his two small beagle dogs – sisters. I had him drop me off at the Brotherhood Bridge. He said there was no way anything there would resemble 70 years ago.

It was no mistake to visit here last. The bridge crossed over the Mendenhall River and a field with the glacier behind it was clearly seen. There was no question in my mind at all that this was the place Sammy took her x-mas card picture.

I took my last picture in Juneau at this place, among the spent fireweed in a slightly swampy field. I imagined Sammy standing in that field dressed up in skins laughing. Wouldn't she have liked to be remembered in this way? I really believe so. (I really wanted to take my picture in that place, but had one picture left and there was just no place and nobody around to take it

The sun set and I caught the bus back to Juneau. It was the last scene that I saw on my trip. I concluded that Sammy had been very happy during her stay in Juneau. Having been to so many of the same places she had been, I felt I understood her better. I couldn't help but feel very happy, too. Maybe the laughter I heard was hers, but maybe it was my own.

Sunny visits Denali in August, 2001

Two years later Sunny returned to Alaska for a week in August 2001. Her mission this time was to investigate and experience Sammy's visit to the interior of Alaska—the Denali and Mount McKinley portion. She felt it might be daunting to travel there alone, so joined up with a group that would provide guides and buses to tour the area. She ended up being in a group of five that included Sunny and two couples. Sunny never felt like she fit into the group nor felt she could search in her own way for Sammy's presence in this rather rigid group experience. Nevertheless, she was able to visit places Sammy had been and identified more of the old pictures from the family album. Among these were those taken at Savage River and Igloo River Camps. She also made contact with Jane Bryant, a photo archivist at Denali National Park who later helped her with other missing pieces to the puzzle.

Sunny did not document this trip in the detailed way she described her trip to Juneau in 1999, but she left notes regarding many of the photos from this area which are enlightening. These photos and notes were included in the Sammy portion above about Alaska.

Sunny returned again to Alaska in 2006.

This time it was to present some of her research to the Alaska Historical Society Annual Meeting in Juneau, Oct. 5-7, 2006. Her paper was entitled, *Two Met in Juneau and Met Their Fate: Hedvig Samuelson and Ann LeRoi.* This paper and slide presentation is still available to view at Sunny's Web site at the University of Minnesota, www.umn.edu/home/sunny, but it is unknown how long this will continue.

During this trip she was able to explore a glacier cave under the Mendenhall Glacier. She met a guy named Dave who took her kayaking directly into the glacier. This was an unexpected and thrilling bonus for this trip. Sammy had no such pictures in her album like this! These are various pictures of Sunny climbing glaciers and kayaking. Following the pictures is a poem he wrote about her.

The Gumshoe and the Glacier

By Dave Lindo, 2006

September in St. Paul, Building 5, Cubical 2732 to be precise,

A frumpy (Ha!) bumpy librarian plans her journey to the ice.

Twas seven years just prior, this same trip ended in defeat,

Like the ancient glacier, an unsuccessful hike left the gumshoe in retreat

Another bout of homework, she did research on the net,

Finding trails to Mendenhall glacier, to be ready as she could get.

After running down the facts, the trip to Juneau seemed in order,

A withdrawal of airline miles got her to southeast Alaska for a quarter.

Despite the fact that her airship arrived quite late at night,

She was determined to be on the trail at first morning light.

Ominous postings warned of bears, Mendenhall wolf, and other critters,

She signed the trailhead registry "solo" and tried to suppress the jitters.

The muddy, mucky march soon became a technical climb,

Sunny Worel

The gumshoe now faced hardships unable to express in rhyme.

Clawing at rock and grit, she scraped forward by her nails,

In case you have not noticed, this gal is not the type who fails!

Five hours later, the so-called trail was just a bit too steep,

That is unless you are the mountain goat she claims to have seen leap.

Descending down an hour, she stopped to eat green apples and cry,

Suddenly beyond the sodden tears appeared this quite peculiar guy.

Black socks with sandals and suspenders raising ski pants to his nipples,

The gumshoe needed a good laugh, smiles poured from her face in ripples.

"I am looking for the glacier," explained the exhausted odd duck,

The two agreed to search together and perhaps multiply their luck.

Talk of secret shortcuts and side trails, "What is that you speak?"

"You mean I hiked all morning and would have walked all week?"

With the gumshoe in the lead, they chose the alternative route,

She seemed confident of success, so who was he to doubt?

"I am not a hiker," she oft humbly would explain,

Easily bounding rock to rock over treacherous terrain.

The day was clear and sunny yet the air began to chill.

We caught a glimpse of glacier as we mounted the next hill.

Another little scramble placed us right beside the ice,

This twelve mile long popsicle made us feel like meager mice.

We popped inside a massive ice cave, three shades of deepest blue.

The camera burned through film, as the gumshoes' dream came true.

The following day kayaks would bring her to the glacial moraine,

Next year she will probably greet the bergs by jumping a freight train.

CHAPTER EIGHT: PHOENIX, AZ

SAMMY AND ANNE LEFT JUNEAU together on the steamship *Admiral Rogers* on Oct. 2, 1930. The women originally sailed for Laguna Beach, California, but stopped at Seattle and other places on the way south, visiting Anne's family and friends. Anne discovered that she had a mild case of tuberculosis, too, when examined by a physician. Doctors in California suggested that the women head for the dry climate of Phoenix, Arizona, to recover.

On Oct. 20, 1930, they spent the first night at the Westward Ho Hotel, but by October 22 had moved into a duplex at 528 W. Portland St. Sammy, in her diary, described it as the "cutest little house." She found a doctor right away in Phoenix, a Dr. Victor Randolph, who first examined her and did some tests. On October 30, he tried to collapse her right lung, but was unsuccessful. Her diary entries show that she was running a high fever for the next couple of weeks. Since Sammy was bedridden, she received a home visit from a radiologist, Dr. Percy Brown, regarding her health. By chance, he met Anne as well at their home. Anne mentioned that she had been seeking employment, and he discussed the possibility of employing her as his X-ray technician at a new clinic that would be opening in January.

That November, Sammy remained in bed under the care of Dr. Randolph, who made home visits to monitor her. Her diary entries reveal her everyday life. There were a few special occurrences. For example, on November 13 she received a package containing books from a man named Tom. This may have been Tom Freylingsen, who she had met on a steamer. She celebrated her twenty-eighth birthday on November 17 in bed receiving packages and letters. Anne worked part time, but was usually home to look after her. Anne read *The Yellow Mistletoe* to Sammy on the November 25 and was home to make a lovely Thanksgiving dinner for them on November 27. They had visitors the following day, a Dr. and Mrs. Mason. Dr. Mason was a brother of Anne's ex-husband. Sammy's diary entries show that she typically spent a great amount of time alone in bed reading, writing in her journal, doing needlework, and corresponding with family and friends. Often she must have been bored since she wrote in her diary, "One day like all the others. How can I fill these pages?" She would note that she washed her hair or received mail. Sammy had been extremely social and outgoing previously, so life was suddenly very different and discouraging for her. On her wall above her bed she had a poem entitled "Say Damn" which must have expressed her feelings at least some of the time.

It does you no good to grow bitter
When Luck up and hands you a slam
Lie Down and you lose as a quitter.
So, just grit your teeth and say damn.[27]

Work was sporadic that fall for Anne, but Dr. Percy Brown did stop by again in December to offer Anne the position as his X-ray technician at the new Grunow Clinic that was opening on Jan. 1, 1931. Since the country was in the midst of the Depression and the women had been living on the dwindling money that had been provided for them to leave Alaska, they were delighted to have more financial security, even though it would mean Sammy would be home alone much of the time.

---

[27] *Murder Mystery Stories Had Thrilled Two Victims of Phoenix Trunk Slayings*, in *Minot Daily News*, Oct 26, 1931: Minot, ND, 3.

Meanwhile another young attractive woman was alone and also financially struggling in Phoenix. She was Winnie Ruth Judd, the daughter of an Indiana minister and the wife of a drug-dependent doctor much older than herself. Dr. William C. Judd had been wounded in World War I and had become addicted to morphine as a result. The Judds had lived in Mexico, where he worked as a doctor for mining companies. Now, however, he was a patient at Whipple, a Veterans Administration hospital in California, where he was being treated for his addiction. Ruth, as she was called, ended up in Phoenix in May 1930 alone, seeking employment and also a climate suitable for her own mild tubercular state. Ruth actually had not planned to live in Phoenix. She had been on her way to Los Angeles when the car of the woman she was traveling with broke down in Phoenix and she decided to stay.[28] She had no money on arrival, and worked in a kitchen for her meals for the first few days. Through the YWCA, she found refuge with the Leigh Ford family, for whom she was employed for a salary plus room and board to care for the ailing Mrs. Ford. She also was to do light housework and help with the three children. The Fords' home was at 29 W. Monroe St. Their next door neighbor was a wealthy married lumberman by the name of Jack Halloran. He was quick to notice Ruth and she often spent evenings sitting outside with him, relating stories about her life in Mexico. By fall, she wanted a better job for herself, since she was also trying to support her husband. She worked for a few weeks at the office of the Maricopa County Physician, Dr. C.W. Brown (not to be confused with Dr. Percy Brown), but he fired her quickly for incompetence. By November she had secured employment as the office nurse of Dr. H. McKeown, a chest expert, for $75 a month. During this period, the Fords continued to let her use a room in their home in exchange for help with the children. Dr. McKeown was planning to move his practice to the Grunow Clinic when it opened in January. He told Ruth she could work there with him if she would learn stenography. She agreed and enrolled in a night school program three nights a week. By mid-December, she had moved into a duplex with Betty Murray, a historian at Good Samaritan Hospital. The residence, known as the Monte Vista duplex, was at 2201 N. Richland St. Ruth led a quiet life, attending school three nights a week, keeping up with washing and ironing the three uniforms she needed for work at the clinic, all that she could afford to buy at the time. Ruth was asked to help prepare dinner at the Ford house that Christmas. Jack Halloran renewed his friendship with her and came to her apartment that evening and an intimacy began between them.

---

[28] Judd, William C, *My Life with Winnie Ruth Judd* – Part 1, *in Intimate Detective Stories*, March, 1940

The Louis Grunow Clinic opened as scheduled at Tenth Street and McDowell right after New Year's 1931. Anne began working in the X-ray department on the very first day. Ruth Judd also began that day working for Dr. McKeown, who was in the process of moving his offices into the new building. Ruth requested to see the entire building. Mrs. Anna Evans, a 50-year-old nurse, led her on a tour and this included the X-ray department. There she met Anne and they talked for a while. Ruth described her experiences in Mexico and Anne talked about her life in Alaska. These were women, you might say, from opposite poles. Since the doctors were always referring cases to X-ray, Ruth often brought patients down there to be cared for by Anne LeRoi and a friendship developed between them. Anne mentioned Sammy and asked Ruth if she wanted to meet her. Ruth was delighted to do so since she had few friends.

Early in January, Dr. Judd left the hospital at Whipple where he had been hospitalized for six months. His doctor declared him cured although he had frequent relapses. He was unemployed and undecided as to what to do. He decided to join Ruth in Phoenix and arrived Jan. 10, 1931. Ruth had by then visited Anne's duplex and met Sammy and by February had brought her husband into this social group. The Judds often visited the two women several times a week. Dr. Judd first lived with Ruth at the duplex with Betty Murray, but on March 1, Ruth rented an apartment at 1130 E. Brill St., Unit C. Ruth kept up her employment and Dr. Judd helped her with the cooking and housework. She encouraged her elderly parents to come out and live with them since she complained about missing them and being nervous.

Life continued much the same for the bedridden Sammy, but with disappointing news. On Feb. 3, 1931, Sammy wrote in her diary, "They say if you lose a friend you die a little. If that is true, part of me is dead."[29] Howard Hagen, her former boyfriend from her year in Landa, North Dakota, now had a wife; their baby was born that February. Later, Sammy got a letter from Clara Bogstie in Landa saying in part, "Suppose you know Howard H. is married and lives in Atlanta, GA, and already has a baby girl."[30]

In April 13, 1931, Howard Hagan wrote Sammy a letter on stationary from the Sun Life Assurance Co. of Canada from Atlanta, Georgia. The letter read, "Dear Sammy: Under separate cover I am sending you today your photograph. I had not thought it would have taken so long to get around to it and so I apologize if it has caused you any concern. It is so beautiful here in Georgia now, I wish you could see all the blossoming trees and shrubs. No doubt Phoenix is radiant too and my

---

[29] *Diary of Murder Victim Bares Loss of Friend*, in *Wisconsin News*, Oct 22, 1931, Milwaukee, WI, 2.

[30] *Intimate picture given of Sammy by Letters*, In *San Francisco Call Bulletin*, October 23, 1931: San Francisco. 1,12.

fervent hope is that you are up and around enjoying it. Please, Sammy, let me know how you're getting on. It's so unkind of you to be so provincial to an old friend because he happens to be married. With best wishes always, I am truly, Howard."[31] It was said that Sammy had written to him of her desire to discontinue their correspondence because of his marriage to another.

On January 4, Sammy copied a quote from Oliver Herford in her diary:

God made man frail as a bubble,

God made love: love made trouble.

God made wine—was it a sin

That man took wine to drown trouble in?[32]

On Feb. 26, 1931, Sammy quoted from Tennyson in her diary: "Oh, let the solid ground not fail beneath my feet before my life has found what some have found so sweet."[33]

 She also wrote: "Behaviorist. I am what I am. I shall do what I shall do because of the Mendelian laws of heredity and the physical reflexes developed in my childhood. This is wisdom—to love—to live, to take

---

[31] *Letters of Friendship to Miss Samuelson Bared*, in *Los Angeles Evening Herald*, Oct. 22, 1931: Los Angeles, 11.

[32] *Trunk Slayer Has Killed Self, Police Believe*, in *Chicago Daily Tribune*, Oct 22, 1931: Chicago, IL.

[33] *Trunk Victim Leaves Weird Diary*, in *Chicago American*. October 21, 1931: Chicago, 3.

what fate the gods may give."[34] This is from Laurence Hope's poem, the *Teak Forest.*

Additionally she wrote, "Now I am a hedonist. Follower of the doctrine that pleasure is the chief end of man."[35]

One of Sammy and Anne's pleasures was to listen to the radio together in the evening, and especially to a Sherlock Holmes radio show that presented murder mystery plays. On March 16 the radio show that was aired was called "Problem of Thor Bridge."

Sammy indicated in a letter to the Bogsties in Landa, North Dakota, in March what a blow it had been to her to discover that she had tuberculosis. She hoped that she could recover soon and be able to explore the desert. She also said she and Anne had plans to visit Mexico or South America someday. She told them about their cute house and her hope to get strong again soon.

Toward the end of April, Sammy and Anne relocated to 2929 N. Second St., a duplex that had a family occupying the other side. Dr. and Ruth Judd continued to visit and moved into the other side less than a month later when the family left. Dr. Judd didn't work but did look after Sammy sometimes in the daytime. At times, Sammy would have him move a cot into the

---

[34] *Trunk Slayer Has Killed Self, Police Believe,* in *Chicago Daily Tribune,* Oct. 22, 1931: Chicago, IL

[35] *Diary of Murder Victim Reveal Hedonistic Lure,* in *Daily Alaska Empire.* Oct. 31, 1931: Juneau, AK 1, 4

vacant lot; she would shield it with a palm leaf sun shade and use it as an arbor. There is a photo of Sammy wearing a Jantzen bathing suit and a large sombrero that is probably from this time, although Sammy looks healthy. By this time, Jack Halloran, the lumberman, had been introduced to Anne and Sammy by Ruth and had become a frequent visitor in their home.

During May, tension began to rise between Anne and Ruth over Jack Halloran's apparent increasing interest in Anne. The Judds traveled to Los Angeles late in May for a funeral. Afterward, Dr. Judd remained in LA for a time with his sister Carrie while Ruth returned alone on June 1. She found both Sammy and Anne sick with fever and attempted to care for them, but was unable to since she had to work. Ruth arranged to have Jack Halloran pay nurses Anna Evans and Evelyn Nace to help out, although Sammy and Anne were unaware of this. Anne was stressed and sick and requested a leave of absence from her employment. She felt she needed to spend time in Oregon with family to regain her health and to escape from growing tensions in Phoenix. Dr. Judd had returned and had begun to drink often with Jack Halloran. This was distressing to Ruth, not only because of her past and possible current romantic interest in Jack, but because of her wish to protect her husband from addiction. Anne was able to find the financial resources to leave by borrowing money in mid-June for a three- month leave. In Portland, Anne's TB was treated by Dr. Ralph Matson. He performed a phrenectomy, a procedure in which a nerve was cut to partially paralyze the diaphragm and diminish the expansion of her diseased lung. She worked for this doctor to pay for her medical treatment.

Back in Phoenix, Sammy was failing and needing more help. Ruth went around evenings looking for a sanitarium that might take her. Mid-June, Sammy moved to the Pearl Waggoner Home, a private sanitarium located at 1821 E. McDowell Road. Sammy improved with the care provided there. She was not forgotten by her friends and had frequent visitors. Ruth visited her two to three times per week, spending 30 cents street car fare to get there, and Pearl Waggoner said that she often drove Ruth home. Nurse Anna Evans visited, as did a Dr. Guttman. Also, Jack Halloran visited and brought Sammy flowers. Once Jack came with three other men and they stayed in Sammy's room and sang songs. Anne wrote to Ruth saying she appreciated her friendship and her attention to Sammy and at times indicated remorse for prior difficult episodes between them.

Dr. Judd and Ruth moved to the other side of the duplex, the side formerly occupied by Sammy and Anne, apparently because the furniture was better. Then Dr. Judd got a job at the Copper Queen Hospital in Bisbee, Arizona. He borrowed money for car fare and left on August 7. He was to be paid $50 a week, but the job was only to last a month, filling a vacancy. Ruth was alone in Phoenix and lacking money. She felt she had to continue her job at the clinic or be completely broke. She could not rejoin Dr. Judd until he made enough to take care of them both. She wrote to Carrie, Dr. Judd's sister, for help, but she, Carrie, had no money either. Ruth simply did not make enough money to live alone in the duplex. Sammy was also having financial worries, which she expressed to Ruth. It cost her $60 a month to remain at Pearl Waggoner's. Ruth suggested that Sammy move in with her to save both of them money. Sammy rather reluctantly agreed after evaluating her own desperate financial situation. Sammy wrote the following letter to Anne between August 11 and 14: "You'll be surprised, pleasantly I don't know however, that I've made my first decision since you put me to bed in Juneau September 25, 1930. Sunday I'm moving luggage and self over to 2929 Second Street again. Wouldn't do this, but $80 per month finances was getting to be a big problem. You will see it this way. Dr. Judd is relieving a doctor at Bisbee for a month and Ruth is by herself. She wants me to come over and stay, and I'm going to try it. I don't like it very much, but it will save half. Now, Honey if you don't want to stay over there with three in a house why I'll do whatever you wish when you get here. I realize it's not going to be the same having three, because I'm a jealous little fool, though I do my best to hide it."[36]

In August Sammy wrote another letter to Anne in Portland: "I am so glad you are feeling better and are coming back. It's foolish to be so dependent on someone for happiness, but how can I help it? Miss Waggoner has been lovely to me, but she doesn't mean anything to me. It's the same way with Ruth. Now honey, please answer this right away so I will know how you are and when you will get here. Ever Yours, Hedvig."[37]

On Aug. 5, 1931, Sammy wrote the following letter to her friend Marion Alvina Vrem, who she had gone to school with in Minot: "I'm sorry to know you have a cold. Be careful of it. Remember that's all the warning I had and I didn't know enough to heed it....Their wives are

---

[36] *Letters Bare Mrs. Judd Drug Bond to Victim*, in *Los Angeles Evening Express*. Oct. 22, 1931: Los Angeles, 4

on the coast, too hot for them here. Papas don't seem to mind the heat somehow. Several of them come over and help me while away the hours, a doctor, lumberman, and a contractor from L.A. building a bank here. It's nice of them because I'm not allowed up, lie out in a swing in the evenings, which doesn't make me very good company, when I can't go places or do things. Also have two girl friends that come over, so you see I'm not altogether forsaken. Yes, you sent me 'Vagabond's House' and I love it. Are you working now? Much love, Sammy."[38]

On August 16, Sammy got positive news about her health and X-rays. She was examined by Dr. Randolph, who said that her left lung had no tubercular activity and that she might be up by Christmas. Dr. Guttman brought her home from the rest home since Ruth had gone to Bisbee to visit her husband. Nurse Anna Evans moved into the opposite side of the duplex to care for Sammy while she was alone. Sammy wrote to her brother saying, "My new x-rays give me a lot of encouragement, so maybe by next spring I'll be out looking for new fields to conquer."[39]

Meanwhile, Ruth was exhibiting strange behavior. She had persistent delusions that she had a child and believed her baby was with Dr. Judd in Bisbee, so she went there to find him. She had also become suspicious that Sammy was trying to take Jack away from her since he

---

[37] Ibid

[38] *Sammy was good pal, says girl*, in *San Francisco Call Bulletin*, Oct. 22, 1931, San Francisco

[39] *Slain Girl's Letters Fail to Solve Mystery*, in *Chicago Daily Tribune*. Oct 21, 1931: Chicago

had visited Sammy at the sanitarium. She had a series of screaming fits she could not control. In Bisbee she signed the registry at the Copper Queen Hotel with the alias "Lucy Rider," called her husband to hear his voice, but would not at first agree to see him. He finally found her and they spent the night together in the hotel, but she stated she had terrible things on her mind and again had screaming episodes. She was taking the drug Luminal, which Dr. Judd warned her would be harmful. When she returned to Phoenix, she had not slept for 36 hours.

On August 20, Ruth wrote Anne a letter; "Dear Anne; I was so glad to get your letter after such a long time. I suppose you know that Sammy and I are together waiting every day for our dear little Anne to return to the fold. Sure I think that we can get along fine, the three of us, until I go live with the doctor. We talk a lot about our Anne and how she is going to behave herself when she comes back. Sammy is flirting as per usual. I went to Bisbee on Saturday and Sammy moved over to the house on Sunday night. A doctor brought her over. He hated to leave her, and frankly told me so the next day. Well, at 5 am Sammy heard someone come in the back door and she got up and ran out to greet the milk man. He was terribly surprised and started to run. Then Sammy told him she thought it was Ruth. I don't know what to believe. Anyhow, the milk man is as sweet as pie and doesn't run any more, but looks forward to these little morning greetings. You know Anne, I sleep so sound that a truck could run in the house and I would never awaken. Sammy also flirts with the ice man. He stands for hours with my ice box door open and talks, so Sammy says. Jack came back from the coast for a couple days and came out to the house. He brought flowers. He's just as sweet as he can be."[40]

On August 23, Sammy wired Anne LeRoi $50 so she could return from Portland. That evening Sammy burst into tears and told Ruth how much she thought of Anne. That she would do anything for Anne but that she was almost broke; that nearly all the money she had received from the people in Alaska was gone; that she would do anything in the world to get Anne back again.

On August 24, Sammy wrote a letter to her sister Anna in Chicago. Part of this letter said, "I hope that everything is all right. Had a dream about you the other night. Dreamt that you gave birth to twins, a boy and a girl. My dream made them look about two months old. A child is something I'll probably never have now. T. B. people haven't any business bringing people into the world. Good thing that has never been my ambition. I'm relieved to know it's all over and you are the proud mother of a big strong son. Now, perhaps, you'll be content to leave some of the slackers to help populate the world. I'm glad that Robert will be dark. They make such handsome men. Ten pounds seems to be an awful lot for a baby to weigh—no wonder you had such a hard time. Just think all the time I've spent in bed! I could have a baby two months old. I moved over here last Sunday. Just seems like coming home after a vacation. It may not be as good for me over here, but I'm happier. Ruth isn't near as good a cook as Anne, but she's sweet. Works as an office nurse at the clinic. Anne will be back in a

---

[40] *Strong Bond of Friendship Shown in Ruth's Letter*, in *Chicago Herald & Examiner*. Oct. 22, 1931: Chicago.

few days now. Poor kid, she only made enough money in Portland to pay her hospital and doctor bills, so I wired her $50 last night to come back."[41]

September brought changes. Anne, after visiting her ex-husband's brother, returned to Phoenix. However, the clinic did not take her back until October 1 since it was having financial problems from lack of patients. Also, the clinic doctors were concerned about her TB and wanted to make sure she was well enough to resume her job. Dr. Percy Brown, who had hired her, advocated for her. During this time, Anne usually did the cooking and Ruth did the dishes. Jack Halloran often arrived after dinner and jealousy again flared up between Anne and Ruth. They argued about other things as well – even about Mr. Cat, Ruth's cat that lived with them. That month while Anne was not working, she called up Ruth at the clinic and suggested Mr. Cat be put down because he was having fits. Ruth felt that they had abused the cat and was irate that they thought he should be killed. He did recover but this caused increased tension.

Meanwhile, Dr. Judd's work at Bisbee had ended. He had traveled to Mexico to look for work, but hadn't found any. Ruth told him her relationship with Anne and Sammy was strained, but he encouraged her to try to stay there while he continued to look for employment. It seemed Ruth was the only one working. Anne was looking for special duty work until she could return to the clinic. Dr. Judd traveled back to Los Angeles and stayed with his sister Carrie while he looked for work

---

[41] *Sister Bares Letters of Dead Girl*, in *Chicago American*, Oct. 21, 1931: Chicago 3, 18.

there. He and Ruth communicated regularly. She must have complained about the girls since he advised her to hide her letters from them. She was communicating that she needed to move away from them and wanted him to come home. Additionally, thinking she might be pregnant by Jack, she confessed her infidelity to her husband. Ruth also wrote a frantic letter to her brother Burton asking him to please come see her at once, but he was too busy. On September 25, Ruth had a menstrual period that lasted 21 days, which she felt was a miscarriage. She had already confessed her infidelity and she had hoped that Dr. Judd might agree to keep the baby as his own. Now, without the pregnancy, she was worried he would reject her. Ruth decided she must move out of the duplex and try to get Dr. Judd to move back to Phoenix.

While Anne had been gone for the summer, four men had proposed to her. Sammy thought she had turned them all down, but one was still a lingering possibility. Emil Hoitola, her fiancé, wrote to Anne on September 19, expressing his love and saying how much he missed her. She wrote back to him on September 23, telling him that Dr. Judd was returning home so Ruth would be leaving them. "It really hasn't worked out so well having three of us. We are very fond of her and she is a sweet girl, but there just seems to be a wrong number when one is used to living by oneself and just one other very congenial one."[42]

By early October, Anne returned to work at the clinic and Ruth moved out of the duplex to an apartment at 1130 E. Brill St. She had lived

---

[42] *Trunk Slaying Motive Sought*, in *Arizona Daily Star*, Oct. 21, 1931: Tucson, 9.

there earlier in Unit C, but now moved into Unit F. In moving there, she may have wanted to be closer to the clinic, but it seems she also wanted to get away from Anne. She rented from Kenneth Grimm, who helped her move, but she left most of her things to move later. She expected Dr. Judd to return, but instead he continued to stay with his sister Carrie. Ruth did take Mr. Cat with her but the cat kept returning to the house on North Second Street and seemed to prefer living with Sammy and Anne, much to Ruth's disappointment. Ruth was continually in an agitated state and needed to take Luminal as a sleeping aid. Her finances were a worry and when $15 disappeared out of her pay, which she had left in her desk drawer at work, she felt desperate. An hour later she received a letter from home saying that her papa had been out chopping wood and that a big limb had fallen on him and broken his ribs. He was in terrible agony. Ruth was frantic with worry and hoped she could get her parents to Phoenix so she could care for them.

Life was better for Sammy and Anne without Ruth. Sammy wrote to her parents: "It was a grand morning, nice and cool. We even used blankets last night. My bedroom is going to be lovely this winter because it faces the east which will give me the lovely morning sunshine. The sun feels good for the first time in months. Ruth moved, so are alone again and we like it so much better. Three never get along very well." She concluded her letter by writing, "We're looking forward to a happy year in Phoenix. Don't feel badly about my having to stay in bed. Why I have it better than most people that are up. Have a nice home to live in, even a telephone by my bed so I can talk in bed as long as I feel like it without getting tired. My doctor thinks he will let me get up at Christmas, which is a very short time considering the year I have already been in bed. Don't worry. It would be different if I felt sick, but I don't."[43] Sammy received another letter from Howard Hagen, who told her about his eight-month-old daughter Ann and tried to give her encouragement. She also wrote to him in October. Anne and Sammy continued to enjoy Sherlock Holmes radio shows. In regard to one of them, she wrote in her diary on October 6: "Turned off the lights and were too scared to sleep."

Dr. Judd, who was still in Los Angeles, was planning to come and live with Ruth, but then a temporary job came up with the chance to earn some badly needed money. He was to work for nine days, from October 11 to October 20. He later regretted this decision thinking he could have averted the upcoming tragedy if he had been with Ruth in Phoenix. By letter he advised her to get hold of herself and quit her medications. "It will knock out your nervous system if you don't cut it out," he said.

Halloran, who had been the cause of so much tension between Ruth and Anne, was still coming around. At 2 a.m. on October 10 he visited Ruth's place drunk and entered with the driver of his taxi. She had just managed to get to sleep. When she awoke, she told him to not visit so late at night. He said that was fine, he would go visit Anne instead.

On October 12, Anne went for lunch at Ruth's new place and got sick after eating Ruth's Mexican cooking. Anne had a fleeting thought that she might have been poisoned. Ruth told Anne that she wanted to get

---

[43] *Stricken Parents Mourn For Girl Slain in West; Pastor Tells Sad Story*, in *Minot Daily News.* October 21, 1931: Minot, ND. 10,

her parents moved to Phoenix and explored the possibility that they could all get a place together to save money. Anne apparently did not turn her down outright, because Ruth began to work with a realtor to find a possible place for all of them.

At work that week, Anne asked office nurse Evelyn Nace for advice on a delicate subject. Suppose, she said, that you had a friend who you knew was going out with someone you knew had a venereal disease, should you tell him? Evelyn said yes. This concerned a woman Halloran wanted to meet. He had asked Ruth for an introduction. Ruth knew the woman had tested positive for syphilis at the clinic but this was confidential and she couldn't tell him. Perhaps Anne didn't want Halloran to get involved with this woman, and perhaps she thought Ruth should put aside the rules of confidentiality and tell him. In any case, the issue seems to have heightened the tension between Anne and Ruth.

The days between October 14 and 16 were a bit confusing. Jack Halloran had business friends in town. They installed a new radio in Anne and Sammy's place but had dinner at Ruth's. Anne invited Dr. Brinkerhoff, a new clinic doctor, over for dinner and he contemplated renting the other half of their duplex. It seemed underlining tensions were present as Anne and Ruth competed for Jack's attention, but they continued to have lunch together and were outwardly cordial. Ruth continued to look for a place for all of them to live. Anne invited Evelyn Nace over on October 16 for dinner and cards after and Anne pressed Ruth to come over too so that they would have enough people for a game of bridge with four players. Ruth asserted she was too busy with work she needed to type at home and did not have time. She actually was hoping that Jack would visit and wanted to be available. As it got late, Ruth became angry when Jack didn't arrive, so she went over to Sammy and Anne's place. Evelyn had gone before she arrived. Somehow during that night or next morning, both Sammy and Anne were shot to death. Ruth was the only one left to explain what happened, and she offered different accounts. What had actually happened was unclear.

Sammy left an unsent letter behind at the duplex for her sister Anna in Chicago. Excerpts from this letter have been printed out of context many times. It is currently stored at the Arizona State Library, Archives and Public Records. Sammy's neat handwriting in this letter matches the writing on some family photos as well as diary entries and a letter published in old newspaper clippings. She certainly wrote this letter. Read as a whole, this letter hinted at her personality and her life on the day she died. October 16, 1931, started like a day like any other for Sammy Samuelson in Phoenix. Nothing much was going on.

Dearest Sis:

I wrote you about a week ago to your old address, so no doubt you didn't receive it. Know how you feel about your new home. Isn't a fireplace the most cheerful thing, if used? Never could understand why people use them as an ornament only. Sunday morning it was a little crispy so we had a fire and placed the bridge table in front of it with our breakfast. Shortly afterwards Mr. and Mrs. Fitchbew (architect for the clinic) took us for a lovely ride. They live across the street from us. Yesterday we received the loveliest surprise. You know we had to give up our Philco Radio, when we both became ill last spring. Well a man that we had only met the day before had a lovely Jackson Bell radio that they had been using for demonstrations came over and presented us with the lovely $50 radio. Its eight tubes and the most wonderful tone I've ever heard. Last night I got Chicago, Cincinnati, Texas, San Fran, L.A., Mexico and Denver. Mr. Ryan is from El Paso Texas, and we very likely won't see him again so there's no strings attached. Wasn't that a lovely thing to do? Of course, he is a man of means, but even at that it was a lovely surprise.

Anne had a small dinner party last night. A new doctor at the clinic was her guest. He's a tall homely chap but an interesting talker and unmarried, which is unusual; almost all the men we've met are married. He's a nose and throat specialist – Name is Dr. Brinkerhoff. He may rent the duplex next to us. So, if he does we will be either friends or enemies by spring.

We are so much happier here by ourselves. Ruth and Anne clashed in many things. We get along so well but it shows there has to be a lot of tolerance which comes from love.

Really Anna there are some people in this world that are so kind that they make up for all the selfish ones. Dear old Capt. Lathrop sent me the sweetest letter wanting me to be sure to write and tell him if I needed financial aid. He will be in Seattle by Nov. 1, but that's a long ways from here.

I'm listening to Montgomery Ward "Beautiful that's" program. N.B.C. from Chicago. I enjoy their 15 min in the air every morning. Seth Parker will be here in person in Nov. Sure wish I could see them, but no chance.

Sure glad Betty (niece) is having a chance to begin music. Disappointed in Robert (newborn nephew) being a blonde but a brunette girl will very likely enjoy his blondness someday.

The weather is lovely now. Soon it will be America's winter playground again.

Much love to you, Hedvig[44]

Sammy appreciated the writings of Don Blanding and especially *Vagabond's Road*:

Not for all the lonely winding road that leads across the hill

Into the neverness beyond. And not for all the restless thrill

Of changing skies. Only for him who knows the ceaseless urge

To go . . . go ever on, carried by tide and trade-winds pulsing surge,

Lured by the bright mirage of far-off places,

Forests and jungles and bleak frozen spaces,

Ready to bid love greeting or farewell

With the same light gesture. Knowing the spell

That makes the Somewhere-else the Promised Land,

Caring no whit if Sun or Surr or Samarkand

Shall bleach his bones or curious creatures of the sea

Play havoc with his flesh. Content to be

Lover of chance with Loneliness for wife,

Faithful to faithlessness of all save life,

Sunny Worel

Ready to face that last dim misted trail

When eager eyes and pliant muscles fail,

Thinking of Death as just another place to go,

Another road to walk, another land to know.[45]

Also this poetry was found in her diary: *Vagabond's House*, also by Don

Blanding: (Hedvig Samuelson's Diary, September 28, 1931)

Philanderer

Love me, Love, But love me lightly.

Weave no silken gauze to tie me.

I acknowledge most contritely

Vows are bonds that irk and try me.

If you find a strand enfolds me,

Flick a careless finger through it.

Break the gossamer that holds me

But, be sure I see you do it.

Then, because I think you flout me,

I will take the bond you sever

And I'll bind it close about me

For a while. . .if not forever.[46]

---

[44] Samuelson, Hedvig, *Correspondence of Hedvig Samuelson to Anna Samuelson*, October 16, 1931, RG107, Box 2, Arizona State Archives, folder labeled Judd Correspondence.

[45] Blanding, Don, *Vagabond's House*, 1928, New York: Dodd Mead & Company

Another book had importance to Sammy. This was *The Ruba'iyat of Omar Khayyam*. Several passages were quoted in her diary:

Ah, with the Grape my fading Life provide,

And wash my Body whence the life has died,

And in a Windingsheet of Vineleaf wrapt,

So bury me by some sweet Gardenside. (LXVII)

That ev'n my buried Ashes such a Snare

Of Perfume shall fling up into the Air,

As not a True Believer passing by

But shall be overtaken unaware. (LXVIII)

Sunny Visits Phoenix

Sunny visited Phoenix many times, often using a condo of her aunt, Kristine Hanlon's, where she could work on this research as well as do her regular work. She visited all the sites where Sammy lived and collected extensive information about Winnie Ruth Judd after the murder.

---

[46] Blanding, *Don, Vagabond's House*, 1928, New York::Dodd Mead & Company.

First photo: The duplex where Sammy and Anne lived, photo taken when Sunny visited in 2010. Second photo: Jack Halloran's house.

In 2008, Arizona State University, in collaboration with PBS, produced a television documentary on Winnie Ruth Judd for a series called Arizona Stories. Sunny participated in this as a victim's relative along with Jana Bommersbach, author, and Jerry Lewkowitz, the son of Ruth's defense attorney. Bill McCune was the documentary producer. This may possibly be viewed on YouTube.

On May 21, 2006, Sunny also presented a paper at the Medical Library Association Annual Meeting in Phoenix. Her paper was entitled "Changing Measures of Madness: The Case of Winnie Ruth Judd." In the paper, Sunny examined the evidence used to attempt to determine the state of Ruth's mental health and noted how perceptions of mental health have changed over time.

Sunny continued her research even on her last visit to Phoenix in 2014, when she was there for several months in a clinical study for her cancer at the Mayo Clinic.

Epilogue

THE WINNIE RUTH JUDD CASE became one of the most notorious and controversial crimes in the history of Phoenix, Arizona. Agnes Anne LeRoi and Hedvig Samuelson were shot and killed, Sammy was dismembered, and the bodies were shipped in trunks to Los Angeles in October of 1931. The court initially found Judd guilty of this crime, acting alone and in sound mind. She was sentenced to hang but was later declared insane, escaping often from the mental hospital, sometimes even for years. Winnie Ruth Judd's true story has merged with folklore in the historical record of Arizona.

The name of Winnie Ruth Judd is still prominent in Phoenix history. Hedvig (Sammy) Samuelson and Anne LeRoi are basically forgotten except by few who remember them as the victims in the trunks.

This book at least gives hints of the real personality of Hedvig Sammy Samuelson. Anne LeRoi's story is remembered by her family but has probably not been recorded.

For further information about Winnie Ruth Judd and the crime, the following sources are suggested:

Dobkins, J. Dwight, *Winnie Ruth Judd: The Trunk Murders*, Grosset & Dunlap: 1973

Bommersbach, Jana, *The Trunk Murderess: Winnie Ruth Judd*, Simon & Schuster: 1992.

Pela, Robrt, Ruthless: *"A Long Lost Confession Letter May Finally Tell the Real Story of Winnie Ruth Judd,"* Phoenix New Times, 9/24/2014.

Pela, Robrt, *"Baggage Claim: One Writes About Murderess Winnie Ruth Judd at One's Own Expense,"* Phoenix New Times. 1/21/2015.

ACKNOWLEDGMENTS

Sᴜɴɴʏ ᴅɪᴇᴅ ʙᴇꜰᴏʀᴇ sʜᴇ sʜᴀʀᴇᴅ thoroughly who was of primary assistance to her in her search for Sammy. However, Sunny's personal papers show that many people did help. Sammy's cousin Inga Betten, who Sunny visited in 1998, would be acknowledged for her gift to Sunny of the Christmas card with the photo of Sammy wearing a coat made of animal skins. Sunny received that card early in her search and the image captured her interest. In addition, Sunny found key people wherever she traveled. Sunny felt so blessed to have met the late Mabel Monson Burford, the teacher who took Sammy's place in Juneau. Mabel was able to paint a picture for Sunny of what Sammy probably experienced while there. Another vital source of assistance was Jane Bryant, a former photo archivist, now retired, at Denali Park in Alaska. She helped Sunny in Sunny's effort to use family photos to identify places Sammy had been. Roy Milligern from the Jefferson County Museum in Whitehall, Montana, helped Sunny find former students of Sammy and provided information about the town of Whitehall. Sunny relied on Wendi Goen from the Arizona State Archives to find her way around the archives and track down information about Sammy's life and the crime. Robrt Pela, columnist for *Phoenix New Times*, shared Sunny's interest in this topic and served as a sounding board for crime theories and possible insights. Sunny also would have acknowledged Dave Lindo, who wrote a poem about her, *The Gumshoe and the Glacier*, and took her kayaking in a glacier cave. But above all, she received great support from Charles Kelly, who wrote the foreword for this book. He avidly shared her interest in this topic, became a friend who helped her with the work, and at times accompanied her to sites related to Sammy or the crime. He was always available to chat with her about any new exciting discoveries she had uncovered. Certainly there were many others Sunny contacted who are unknown.

Charles Kelly became instrumental, as well, to Janet Worel, Sunny's mother, who called him for advice on how to self-publish the nearly completed book. He volunteered to take on the essential task of editor and formatter of this document. Under his scrutiny, the book became a polished work in which she could feel pride. Charles had the contacts and experience that Janet lacked, and became a trusted partner. He had a knack for gently changing Janet's language to interconnect parts of the book, while being respectful in keeping Sunny's diary entries intact to preserve the unique flavor of her language and spirit.

Janet was delighted with the book cover created by J. T. Lindroos. His masterful art work captured the very essence of the book.

Janet acknowledges Dian Darby, the daughter of Arnold Samuelson, for sharing Arnold's diary and giving permission to use quotes in this book. Though Sunny referred to him as a jerk, his daughter noted that he relished that designation.

Janet's family members are also acknowledged for their patience and assistance with this project. Janet's sister Phyllis Peterson did genealogical research that was used in writing the history of the Samuelson family in the chapter about White Earth. Janet's sister Nancy Dokken played a huge part in contacting Arnold Samuelson many years ago, asking for information about Sammy's murder. Although she had to endure Arnold's wrathful comments about her "blood-thirsty" interest in the crime, she nudged him into sharing facts and insights about the family that otherwise would have been lost forever. Both sisters and Janet's husband Jack were helpful in reviewing and giving encouragement during the writing phase. Janet's granddaughter, Greta Worel, was helpful in suggesting cover design. Janet's son Ben made a key contribution early on when Janet mentioned her intention of writing about Sammy. He said he was most interested in Sunny's search for Sammy. This caused Janet to change the focus of the book to include Sunny's life and her search as well as Sammy's story. He was right. Both the Sammy and Sunny stories needed to be told and preserved.

ABOUT THE AUTHORS

SUNNY LYNN WOREL WORKED independently as a Medical Information Specialist starting in 2002. She specialized in online data literature searches of biomedical data bases. She earned her B.S. degrees in Biochemistry and Microbiology from the University of Minnesota in 1990. She received her Masters of Library and Information Science in 1996 from Dominican University/College of St. Catherine and was a senior member of the Academy of Health Information Professionals (AHIP). She belonged to the Medical Library Association (MLA) and the Association of Independent Information Professionals (AIIP). She successfully combined her work over the last 15 years of her life with her passion for her search for Hedvig (Sammy) Samuelson, her great aunt. Sunny died in 2014.

Janet V. Worel lives in a Minneapolis suburb with her husband Jack. She is Sunny's mother and Sammy was her aunt, her father Samuel's sister. Janet and Jack have a son Ben who lives near them with his wife Linda and their two daughters; Anna and Greta. Janet, now retired, worked primarily as a hospice nurse during her years of employment. Sunny and Jan are shown on a swing along with Sunny's beloved dog, Thumper.